7617

This book

Past-into-Present Series

POLITICAL PARTIES

Peter Lane

Principal Lecturer in History,
Coloma College of Education

B. T. BATSFORD LTD London

First published 1972
© Peter Lane 1972

Filmset by Keyspools Ltd, Golborne, Lancashire
Printed in Great Britain by The Anchor Press Ltd, Tiptree, Essex
for the Publishers
B. T. Batsford Ltd, 4 Fitzhardinge Street, London W1

ISBN 0 7134 1774 9

7617

320

Contents

Acknowledgment

The Author and Publishers would like to thank the following for the illustrations which appear in the book:

The British Museum for fig. 54; the Bodleian Library for fig. 2; the Central Office of Information for fig. 46; Central Press Photos for fig. 33; the Daily Herald for figs. 43, 61 and 65; Fox Photos for figs. 35 and 62; the Greater London Council for fig. 20; Illustrated London News for figs. 14 and 48; the Imperial War Museum for fig. 32; Keystone Press for figs. 36, 49–51 and 66; the Labour Party Press Service for figs. 25, 34, 38 and 44; the Mansell Collection for figs. 17 and 58; the National Portrait Gallery for figs. 3–6, 7 and 8; Paul Popper Ltd. for figs. 60–61; the Press Association for fig. 68; Radio Times Hulton Picture Library for figs. 1, 13, 19, 27, 52, 53, 57, 63 and 70; Sir John Soane's Museum for fig. 11; the South African Information Service for fig. 74; Sport and General Press Agency for figs. 42 and 47; Sun for fig. 41; Thompson Newspapers Ltd for fig. 40; Topical Press for fig. 45; United Press International for fig. 71.

The Illustrations

1 Origins of Political Parties – the Seventeenth Century

Did you see the headline:

> 'LABOUR PARTY LEADER ATTACKS CONSERVATIVE PARTY'S ECONOMIC POLICY'?

or the one which ran:

> 'TORY LEADER ATTACKS LABOUR'S DEFENCE POLICY'?

If you did not see these two particular ones, you have seen others like them, and have seen or heard on TV politicians from different Parties attacking their opponents, while defending their own policies.

But it was not always like this. In Henry VIII's time, for example, there were no political parties with different party policies. There was only the King's government, the King's Ministers and the King's policy. When and why did it change? When and why did men form political parties? Are our present-day parties the same as the first ones or are their policies different from those of the first political parties?

Uncertainty

Very learned historians such as G. M. Trevelyan and Keith Feiling differ as to when British MPs first formed political parties. They agree that while the King ruled without Parliament then there was no chance for MPs to form parties – whose aim was (and is) to control both Parliament and the government.

The quarrel between Parliament and the Crown began in Queen Elizabeth I's reign and although she had resisted the Parliament's demand that she should marry, she had to give in to its demands on some things – such as trading monopolies. The quarrel about 'Who is to rule, King or Parliament?' boiled up into a

1 When Parliament tried to assert its power in 1642, King Charles I led an armed force into the House of Commons to try to arrest the five leaders of anti-Royalist opinion. This was the final step on the road to Civil War – a first step on the road to the formation of political parties.

I would willingly make a visite to my sister at
Tunbridge for a night, or two at farthest, when do
you thinke I can best spare that time?

I know no reason why you may not for such
a tyme, (2. nights) go the next weeke,
about Wensday, or Thursday, and when no tyme
enough for the adiournement: which you ought
to be the weeke following.

I suppose you will goe with a light
Trayne.

I intend to take nothing but my night bag.

yet, you will not go without 40. or 50.
horse.

I counte that parte of my night bag.

2 Notes passed between Charles II and
Clarendon at a Council meeting. The
King had the right to appoint and later,
to dismiss, Clarendon and until the King
had less power there could be no real
political parties.

Civil War in 1642 [Picture 1] and by 1660 it seemed as if the struggle had ended
in a victory for Parliament. However, in 1660 Charles II was recalled to the
throne, with power to appoint Ministers, to call elections whenever he liked, and
to decide which Bills should become law. More important was the power that
the King had of controlling elections – by using bribery or threats to get the
voters to support his candidate [Chapter 3, Picture 11].

Court and country parties

Charles II with Clarendon as his Chief Minister [Picture 2], followed a moderate
policy – by which the King tried to persuade rather than force Parliament to
pass whatever laws he proposed to them. Some Royalists thought that Clarendon
hadn't gone far enough; they wanted the King to exercise power as the Tudors
had done: they preferred to forget the Civil War and the execution of Charles I.
In 1667 they persuaded Charles II to get rid of Clarendon and appoint Clifford
as his Chief Minister. Clarendon then led a group of MPs in the Commons who
tried to use their power to prevent the King and his ministers doing anything

rash. But they were not a political party in our sense. They were not trying to persuade electors to support them and drive the King's Ministers out of office. They agreed that the King and his Supporters (or Court Party) had the right to govern and that the rest of the nation (represented by Clarendon and his Country Party) had the duty to obey.

Religion and politics
In 1673 Charles II appointed Danby as his Chief Minister. He was in favour of allowing non-Anglicans equal civil and political liberty with Anglicans. In particular, he was in favour of allowing Roman Catholics the right to vote, become members of Parliament, sit on town councils, go to Universities, become judges, and so on. This caused a former Minister, Shaftesbury, to become an opponent of Charles II; while Shaftesbury favoured freedom for Nonconformists, he was opposed to such freedom for Roman Catholics. In 1678 Titus Oates accused the Catholics of a plot to kill the King, burn down London and slaughter the leading Protestants. This accusation led to panic among Protestants which resulted in the execution of many innocent Catholics. In 1685, Oates – found guilty of perjury – admitted that he had invented the idea of the plot. But the damage had been done; in the popular mind the Catholics were labelled 'plotters'. When Louis XIV of France expelled the Protestants from his country in 1685, English Protestants ignored the proof of Oates's perjury: they preferred to imagine that the Papists were out to undo the work of the Reformation.

The Exclusion Bill
Following the revelations of Titus Oates in 1678 there were three quick elections, each of which gave the King and his Ministers a fright because many of his supporters lost their seats to more Protestant candidates. However, this did not mean that the Protestants could form the government – modern politics had not yet begun. What they did was to put forward an Exclusion Bill under which James, the Duke of York and Charles II's successor to the throne, would not be allowed to become King because he was suspected of being a Roman Catholic [Picture 3]. They proposed that Charles II's illegitimate son, the Duke of Monmouth, should succeed.

The first signs of party
Charles II persuaded his supporters in the House of Lords to throw out this Bill. He dissolved Parliament and called for another election. Shaftesbury, the leader of the Protestants, formed the Green Ribbon Club in London which served as the headquarters for his supporters. He and his followers wrote and printed election manifestos, they chose and supported candidates for a number of constituencies,

9

3 James, Duke of York, later King James II. He was an ardent Roman Catholic, and Shaftesbury and the Whigs proposed an Exclusion Bill to keep James off the throne. In a sense, James can be considered a founder of our modern political system.

founded and supported local newspapers through which they could get at the voters. During this period of three elections (1678–81) the political debate on the rights and wrongs of the Exclusion Bill, the arguments for and against having a Catholic King, and the reasons for and against allowing a group of MPs to have power over the Crown, went on in the streets, the coffee houses and the homes of the well-to-do voters.

In some ways the arguments were similar to those of 1641–42 when the struggle between the King and Parliament had ended in the Civil War and the execution of Charles I. This time, 1679–81, the argument was carried on without a war – it

4 William III and Queen Mary were invited to become joint rulers of Great Britain and Ireland. This invitation showed that the politicians had already grown stronger, while the Crown had lost power.

was carried out by politicians who formed themselves into parties. Those who favoured the Exclusion Bill were nicknamed Whigs; this was meant as a slander on them since the Whigs were Scottish rebels who had attacked Edinburgh in 1648. In their turn they nicknamed the King's supporters Tories – an anglicised version of an Irish word meaning a plundering outlaw.

Parties unite

In the late seventeenth century Britain was a thinly populated, mainly agricultural country where a few local nobles and landlords had most of the wealth and most of the political power. The great majority of the people had little interest in the political debate – although the politicians could always arouse the support of the masses in defence of their religion. However, this was always liable to backlash on the politicians. In 1683 some former Roundhead (Parliamentarian) soldiers were found guilty of a plot to kill Charles II and his brother in Rye House. This Rye House plot was used by the Tories to whip up popular support and sympathy for the King. Many towns were deprived of their voting rights so that when James II came to the throne the majority of the MPs were either Tories or willing to support the Tories.

However, not even they were prepared to support the Catholic policies of James II and in 1688 three leading Tories and four leading Whigs sent an invitation to William and Mary [Picture 4], asking them to come over to England to assume the throne. Some Tories continued to support James II through the brief period of war which followed William's landing at Torbay in 1688; the country as a whole supported the Protestant Glorious Revolution which firmly established that Parliament and Crown were partners in the business of government.

2 The Rise of Parties

Parties in the eighteenth century
Both Whig and Tory parties had been formed by MPs to support, or oppose, the Exclusion Bill. By working together a group of MPs (e.g. the Whigs) hoped to be able to persuade the voters to elect other Whigs, and then to use their power in Parliament to force the King to follow a certain policy. However, it has to be remembered that in the eighteenth century – indeed until 1885 – there were no elections in most constituencies, a candidate was returned 'unopposed'. The duty of returning the candidate might have been the privilege of the local land-owner or a small group of councillors, or an equally small group of freemen. We will look at the question of the electorate and elections in Chapters 7 and 8; here we have to remember that there was no need for political parties to go into action in constituencies where candidates were unopposed.

Even in Parliament there was very little evidence of political parties as we understand them. Most MPs were irregular attenders at the Commons: some didn't appear at all in the winter, when travel was dangerous and difficult; others attended for a few days at a time while they enjoyed a few weeks' visit to London, using the Commons as a sort of club; others became MPs until they succeeded to a title and went on to the House of Lords. By far the largest group of regular attenders were the country gentlemen who had no ambition for power or position but thought it their duty to represent their locality at Westminster so that the needs of their locality could be attended to. These squires and merchants were more interested in, say, the building of a fishing quay at Yarmouth than in the party struggles. They were prepared to support whatever Minister was in power – until he offended them when they were quite prepared to switch their support to another Minister.

There was, of course, a small group of full time attenders, almost professional politicians, who wanted power and enjoyed using it. The Pelhams, the Walpoles and Townshends, Stanhopes, Carterets and other families were forever falling into and out of office, winning or losing the support of the majority of Members [Picture 5]. If there were political groupings in the eighteenth century they were loose groupings around a particular leader – so that there were Grafton Whigs, and Rockingham Whigs, Newcastle supporters and Foxites. Some of these groupings were strengthened by ties of blood or marriage but were quite easily loosened to allow Ministers to desert one Chief Minister and join his successor. There were indeed almost as many Tory ideas as there were Tories and almost as many Whig principles as there were Whigs. This looseness lasted well into the

The Stature of a
Great Man or the English Colossus.

5 This is a cartoon produced in 1740; its caption reads: 'The Stature of a Great Man or the English Colossus'. Walpole's opponents resented the power which he had as 'Prime Minister'.

nineteenth century when we find Huskisson's supporters joining the Canningite Tories to throw Wellington and his Tories out of office in 1830, to put in Grey and his Whigs who invited a Tory, Palmerston, to become Foreign Minister. Even as late as 1846 Cobden, a leading member of the Whig–Liberal opposition, was inviting Peel, the Conservative–Tory Prime Minister, to leave the party and form a new grouping to get Free Trade through Parliament.

The Glorious Revolution of 1688–89 had left the monarch free to choose his or her Ministers. Queen Anne [Picture 6] began the practice of choosing all the Ministers from one particular group of politicians – sometimes she chose all Whigs, at another time she chose all Tories. When George I came to the throne in 1714 he believed that the Tories were prepared to support the claims of the Stuarts to the English throne. This drove George I to choose his Ministers from among the leading Whig politicians. Because of his inability to speak English fluently, as well as his unwillingness to try and understand the process of government in his new country, he gave up attending the meetings of his Cabinet so that one of his Ministers had to take the chair, had to act as a link between the King and the Ministers, and so the office of Prime Minister was accidentally invented. George I gave Number 10 Downing Street to Robert Walpole who became his Prime Minister in 1721, and this has been the official residence of the Prime Minister ever since. [Chapter 9 Picture 61.]

6 Queen Anne, who sometimes chose Tories and sometimes chose Whigs to form her governments. She did not try to rule without them – as Charles I had done.

7 John Churchill, later Duke of Marlborough. He was first a Tory supporter of James II, then a supporter of the Whig William III, showing that party loyalties were not very strong in the early days.

Walpole and the Whigs

Walpole governed from 1721 until 1742, and after him the Pelham family maintained Whig governments until 1760. Walpole and, after him, the Duke of Newcastle (Henry Pelham) used the power of the Crown and government to win elections and to gain the support of more MPs. Sir Lewis Namier's book: *Politics at the accession of George III*, contains dozens of examples of the ways in which MPs were rewarded for supporting the government of the day. However, Walpole and his Whig successors were careful not to offend the independent and non-political majority of MPs. Whenever they showed opposition to a Bill it was withdrawn: whenever they demanded action it was taken – even when the Prime Minister thought the action to be stupid, as did Walpole over the war against Spain which began in 1739 in response to demands by the majority of MPs.

Bolingbroke and the Tories

While the few Whig politicians exercised power and enjoyed government the handful of Tory MPs were unable to do much. Up to 1714 they had had their turn at government; under the Hanoverians they had no share. This led to their leader, Bolingbroke [Picture 8], writing a number of books attacking the idea of Party government. The most famous of these books, *The Patriot King*, outlined an idea of government which was later taken up by George III who became King in 1760. Briefly, his idea was that the King – and not a Prime Minister – should govern, and that the King should choose his Ministers from among politicians of all or of no party. As Bolingbroke wrote:

> Instead of abetting the divisions of his people he will endeavour to unite them, and be himself the centre of their union; instead of putting himself at the head of one party in order to govern his people he will put himself at the head of his people in order to govern, or more properly to subdue, all parties. Now, to arrive at this desirable union, and to maintain it, will be found more difficult in some cases than in others, but never impossible, to a wise and good prince.

Opposition

If Bolingbroke's idea of government was right, then the King was to be regarded as the fatherly head of a family united by a common interest and sharing a common idea. The King represented the national interest and to oppose him and

8 Bolingbroke, a leading Tory politician and writer. He believed that the King had the right to choose Ministers without looking at their Party labels. George III tried to do this. His failure was a decisive step along the road to party-political government.

9 When the American colonists succeeded in their war against Britain, George III's government became unpopular. This led to the fall of Lord North's government, and the end of George III's attempt to 'rule without party'.

his government could be seen as opposing the national interest – which ·was almost treasonable.

George III succeeded to the throne in 1760 and began to put Bolingbroke's ideas into practice. He dismissed the long-serving Whigs from office, appointed his former tutor (Bute) as Prime Minister and used his power and influence to build up support for his Ministers. There was little opposition to his attempts – after all he was merely exercising powers given to the Crown by the Settlement of 1688–89. But when his government became involved in the war with the American colonists [Picture 9], there were a number of leading politicians prepared to lead an opposition to the government. Chatham and his supporters, Rockingham and his followers, as well as the Foxites, were united in opposing George III's American policy. This lead to the passing in 1780 of Dunning's resolution that the power of the Crown 'had increased, is increasing and should be diminished'. In 1782 Lord North, the last of George III's personal Prime Ministers, was dismissed and the accession of the Younger Pitt in 1783 marks a new stage in the development of Party government.

10 Cobden was one of the leaders of the Anti-Corn Law League. Although a member of the Whig-Liberal opposition he succeeded in persuading many Conservative-Tories to support his ideas. Party loyalties were still not very strong. However, Disraeli (in the bathing hut) refused to be persuaded. He stayed behind to found a new Conservative Party.

Definition of Parties

Some people have misread Sir Lewis Namier's work and concluded that there were no political parties in the eighteenth century. This would have surprised a number of eighteenth century politicians and observers – including Dr Samuel Johnson, who wrote that the first Whig was the Devil. What is true is that there were no party organisations as we understand them. It is also true that there was little party discipline among MPs. But in 1770 Edmund Burke, a leading member of the Rockingham Whigs, wrote *Thoughts on the Present Discontent* in which he argued that political parties were an essential and natural part of politics. Men, said Burke, do not always act as individuals. They had opinions, ideas and beliefs in common with other people and by acting together, in a party, they would be better able to achieve the aims they had in common. This does not mean that members of a political party share every belief of every other member of that party. Some will believe more or less passionately in certain things: some members of a party will in fact be opposed to some of the ideas of other members of that party. But the ideas that they have in common outweigh the ideas on which they are opposed.

Party and Reform

Burke was ahead of his time in presenting the argument for political parties. No party could hope to gain power until the power of the Crown had been diminished: no opposition party could hope to replace the government party until the electoral system had been reformed.

The first major reform of the electoral system was made in 1832 (Chapter 8). One result of this reform was a large increase in the number of electors so that the old methods of controlling the elections and the voters (Chapter 7) would not be sufficient to control the much larger numbers. It became essential for the parties to get their supporters on the Register of Electors; many of them might not know how to do this or might forget to do it. Local Associations were formed by both Whigs and Tories to get their supporters on to the Registers and to challenge the claims of their rivals. To co-ordinate the activities of these local associations the Tories set up a headquarters at the Carlton Club, and the Whigs set up the Reform Club, in London.

With national headquarters, hundreds of local associations and a national system of communications, the mid-nineteenth century provided the setting for the development of political parties. But until 1885 most elections were un-contested: the parties remained under the national and local control of the aristocracy. We have to look to the Anti-Corn Law League and the Irish for the best examples of political organisation.

3 The Changing Nature of Tory and Liberal Parties after 1867

The mass electorate

When only about 300,000 people voted (Chapter 6) then the party leaders and MPs could manage to control the voters, even when elections were contested. There were a few voters, to be bribed, forced or otherwise persuaded to vote in a certain way [Picture 11]. The number of voters was increased in 1832 and this, as we saw in Chapter 2, led to a change in party organisation. However, in 1867 the Reform Act gave the vote to about two million town dwellers – most of them the better paid working class. This Act did not change the method of voting which still remained open and left the voter exposed to persuasion by an employer

11 Part of a series drawn by Hogarth on the subject of Elections. The candidates and their friends sat beneath their different flags. The voters climbed the stairs to the Returning Officer, whose Polling Book (bottom right) showed the list of voters. The crowd beneath waited to hear the voter's decision and then carried him away – either for more rejoicing or to the river. In the background another voter is being brought across the bridge to the polling station.

NORTH EASTERN RAILWAY.
DARLINGTON SECTION

THE ELECTIVE FRANCHISE.

The Committee hereby inform the Officers and Workmen in their employ, that in Voting at the coming General Election, they are at liberty to act according to their own opinions, and that in doing so their position with the Company will not in any way be affected. The Committee also forbid Canvassing on the Railway Company's premises, by or on behalf of Candidates.

(Signed),

HENRY PEASE, Chairman.
THOS. MAC NAY, Secretary.

Railway Office,
    Darlington, July 22nd, 1868.

WILLIAM DRESSER, GENERAL PRINTER, 41, HIGH ROW, DARLINGTON.

12   Not all employers were as open-minded as this.

[Picture 12] although there were now too many voters for parties and candidates to be able easily to afford to bribe or force them. The Ballot Act 1872 (Chapter 7) almost ended the danger of any outsider affecting the ways in which people voted – although even in the 1890s employers in North Wales dismissed and evicted all their workmen after an election in which the employers' nominee did not get elected.

With an increase in the number of voters and the onset of secret voting, both Conservative and Liberal Parties turned to improving their party organisations in the hope that this would help them to win elections and so gain control of the Parliament and government – which is the main aim of political parties.

Conservative organisation

On 12 November 1867 representatives of 55 constituencies met in the Freemasons Tavern, London, under the chairmanship of John Gorst, MP, to 'consider by what organisation we may make Conservative principles effective among the masses'. Following this meeting there was formed the National Union of Conservative and Constitutional Associations. Every local Conservative Association could join the Union on paying one guinea per year. The functions of the Union were outlined by H. Cecil Raikes, Chairman from 1869 to 1874. He is reported as saying that:

> We had now outlived the time of great family influences and also that period which succeeded the first Reform Bill, which might be called the period of middle-class influence in boroughs. We were living in a day in which the people were to be applied to in a much more direct, clear and positive manner than was the case under the older forms of the constitution, and, therefore, any party who wished to retain their hold upon the country must ascertain how far their proceedings were in harmony with the wishes of the people.

However, Raikes went on to explain that the Union was not trying to take the place of the Party leaders:

> Complaints were made that it did not do all that it ought to do: but he pointed out that it was often suggested that it should do things which did not belong to its peculiar line of duty. The union had been organized rather as what he might call a handmaid to the party than to usurp the functions of party leadership.

The Second Reform Act, 1867, had been passed by Disraeli's government [Picture 13]; he hoped that the workers, in gratitude, would vote for Tory candidates–so he called for an election in 1868. However, the workers voted Liberal and Gladstone became Prime Minister for the first time. In 1872 Disraeli made a

13 The middle-class leader of the aristocratic Tories who hoped to persuade the new working-class voters to 'Vote Tory'.

speech at the Crystal Palace in which he said:

The Tory party, unless it is a national party, is nothing. It is not a confederacy of nobles, it is not a democratic multitude; it is a party formed from all the numerous classes in the realm – classes alike and equal before the law, but whose different conditions and different aims give vigour and variety to our national life.

But he had little influence on his colleagues. *The Times* wrote that he was:

discerning in the inarticulate mass of the English populace the Conservative working man as the sculptor perceives the angel prisoned in a block of marble.

Following his defeat in 1868 Disraeli established the Conservative Central Office to act as a centre for the Party's funds, to prepare election propaganda for the Party's candidates and to prepare pamphlets and notes which could be used by MPs in the Commons and by candidates in the constituencies. In 1872 the National Union of Conservative Associations moved its headquarters into the same building in which the Central Office was already established. Here was the 'nuts and bolts' centre of the Party although the Party leaders continued to make their headquarters at the Carlton Club.

Conservative policy

With the increase in the number of working class voters, there was a shift in Conservative policy. Disraeli had already written his novels in which he outlined the theory of Tory Democracy by which the upper classes would use their political power to make life better for the lower classes. Between 1874 and 1880 Disraeli's government, under the influence of an active Home Secretary – Richard Cross – passed a series of laws which aimed at making life better for the ever increasing number of townspeople. Alexander MacDonald, one of the first working class MPs, said that the Tories had done more for working people in six years than the Liberals had done in half a century.

Disraeli also laid the foundations for the Imperialist policy, which later Conservative governments continued to make their own. He favoured expansion of British colonies in Africa and Asia which pleased the British people who later were to sing 'Land of Hope and Glory' with its line 'Wider still and wider shall thy bounds be set', and to read the poetry of Kipling and Newbolt who wrote in glowing terms of the Empire. The Imperialist policy was opposed by the Liberals but brought many benefits to the British merchants and work people who found expanding markets for their products. Unfortunately it also led to frequent colonial wars in India and Africa as well as in more serious wars such as those against the Boers, while envy of the British was one of the reasons for the growing hostility between Britain and her European rivals.

Finally Disraeli brought the widowed Queen Victoria back into public life and gave her the title: 'Empress of India'. The Queen had once favoured the Whigs under Lord Melbourne and disliked Peel and the Tories. She now became a supporter of Disraeli and his party, disliking Gladstone 'who treats me like a public meeting'.

Liberal policies

In 1867 the debate on the Second Reform Bill showed how loose were party ties. Disraeli was opposed in his Cabinet by Viscount Cranborne who resigned rather than support the Bill, although later, as Lord Salisbury, he became Disraeli's Foreign Secretary. On the Liberal side Gladstone was opposed by

Robert Lowe who feared that a mass, democratic electorate would mean that politicians would lose their influence. Equally, Gladstone – who favoured the Reform Bill – was opposed by Cobden, a radical MP who also feared the effects of an electorate which was, in the main, uneducated [Picture 14].

However, once the Reform Bill had gone through and the Liberals had won the 1868 Election, Gladstone and his government set in train a series of reforms which earned for this Ministry the title: 'The Great Reforming Ministry'. They ended the old system of recruitment and promotion in the Civil Service which had favoured the relatives of the aristocrats and began the present system of examinations by which entrance and promotion are dependent on ability. This pleased the middle classes whose children were going to one or other of the new public schools where they received the same sort of education as the sons of the aristocracy at their older public schools. The middle classes also welcomed Gladstone's reform of the Army, in which promotion was to be on merit and could not be bought, and his University reforms which said that undergraduates did not have to be members of the Anglican Church. These reforms favoured the Nonconformist middle classes who had got the vote in 1832 and had used their power to break the economic power of the aristocrats in 1846 when they forced the repeal of the Corn Laws through Parliament.

14 Gladstone was the first political leader to travel around the country on an electoral campaign Here he can be seen leaving West Calder.

Liberal organisation

The Birmingham Liberal Association was formed in 1865 by William Harris who hoped to so organise the city that Liberals would be returned for all three seats. In 1873 this Association was taken over by two remarkable men: Francis Schnadhorst, a draper and a Nonconformist who became Secretary of the Birmingham Liberal Association in 1873, and Joseph Chamberlain, a Unitarian and a rich manufacturer who had become prominent in the fight for free, compulsory and non-sectarian education. Under these two men the Association became highly organised and efficient. The Association was based on the wards: every resident could become a member of a ward Association for a shilling per year. The ward members elected a ward committee which had the power to co-opt other members. The ward committee officers plus three other members of the ward committee went on to the city executive committee, and since there were 16 wards this meant that there were 80 members who were allowed to co-opt another 30 members. This executive committee plus 30 members from each of the 16 wards (a total of 480) made a general committee of 590, so that the committee was usually known as 'The Six Hundred'. Finally, this committee elected four people to join seven persons nominated by the executive committee as a committee of management, popularly nicknamed 'The Council of Ten'. On the surface this was a democratic organisation. In fact, Schnadhorst, Chamberlain and their friends always managed to get their supporters either elected or co-opted, so that they exercised a tight control over the machine.

In 1877 Schnadhorst and Chamberlain called a meeting of about 100 other Liberal organisations and set up the National Federation of Liberal Associations, which hoped that:

> The essential feature of the proposed federation is the principle which must henceforth govern the action of Liberals as a political party – namely, the direct participation of all members of the party in the direction of its policy, and in the selection of those particular measures of reform and of progress to which priority shall be given. This object can be secured only by the organization of the party upon a representative basis: that is, by popularly elected committees of local associations, and by the union of such local associations, by means of their freely chosen representatives, in a general federation.

Party Leaders and Party Organisations

Both the Conservative and the Liberal Parties now had efficient and democratic Associations. Both parties now had to face a period of struggle between the leaders of the parties and the leaders of the Associations. Chamberlain wanted to challenge Gladstone as leader of the Liberal Party; he wanted to force the Liberal Party to adopt more socialist policies – pensions, unemployment benefit, perhaps a health service – all of which Bismarck had already introduced in

Germany [Picture 15]. When Gladstone showed in 1886 that he and he alone would determine Liberal policy, Chamberlain resigned from the Cabinet and took his followers into opposition. In the 1890s these Liberal Unionists formally joined the Conservative Party and Chamberlain became Colonial Secretary. He later helped to split the Conservative Party in 1904 and so helped the Liberals to win the 1906 election. [Chapter 5, Picture 28]

In the Conservative Party, Lord Randolph Churchill – a younger son of the Duke of Marlborough and father of Winston Churchill – tried to force the Conservative Party to follow the line of social reform that had been laid down by

15 The party leaders were challenged in the 1880s by ambitious rebels. Chamberlain was a radical who wanted Gladstone to adopt a socialist policy – or resign. Lord Randolph Churchill hoped to inherit Disraeli's position as leader of a Radical government. Neither rebel succeeded; party discipline had already become too strong.

THE POLITICAL POLO MATCH.

Disraeli. Churchill's slogan was: 'Trust the people' and he tried to use his leadership of the Conservative National Association to force Lord Salisbury to give him his head. Salisbury, who had himself quarrelled with Disraeli when the latter introduced the Second Reform Bill, refused to be bullied and when Lord Randolph resigned from the Cabinet the Party preferred to follow the leader and not the rebel.

Socialism

By the end of the nineteenth century there was an evident need for the government to play a more active part in the social and economic life of the people. Throughout the nineteenth century governments had tried to make conditions in towns and factories better, but had done almost nothing for people as individuals. By the end of the century a number of writers and speakers – in churches and chapels, newspapers and books – were asking that the government should do something for the old, the unemployed, the sick, the widowed and orphaned. Radicals in both major parties saw the need for such action but until 1906 party leaders were less willing to listen. However, in 1906 the Liberals won a sweeping election victory and under the influence of Lloyd George passed a series of Acts which laid the foundations for the Welfare State. [Picture 16]

28

However, although the Liberals had begun to move in a socialist direction [Picture 17], they had moved too late and were moving too slowly. The needs of the less well off members of society had already led to the formation of the Labour Party (Chapter 4).

17 Among the first to benefit from the new Liberalism were the Old Age pensioners. Here, a husband and wife are filling in the forms to claim the first Old Age Pensions of 5s a week each.

4 The Labour Party

New parties

The Conservative and Liberal parties had their origins, as we have seen, in the religious–political struggles of the seventeenth century, and were started by MPs inside Parliament who wanted to win support from electors outside Parliament. The Anti-Corn Law League (1838–46) was one example of a group which began outside Parliament but which managed to put pressure on MPs inside Parliament so that the Corn laws were repealed in 1846. The Irish were another example of a group of electors who had no representation inside Parliament at first but who managed to organise a political party which by the 1880s had about 80 MPs inside the Commons where they used their influence to get the government to pass laws favourable to the Irish [Picture 18].

18 The Irish voters were wooed by the Liberals (who promised Land Acts and an improvement in life) and by the Land League which wanted to drive the English landowners out of Ireland.

19 By 1870 thousands of skilled workers had a high standard of living due to regular employment, high wages and falling prices.

Working class voters

In 1867 about two million skilled workers were given the vote while about six million more were given the vote in 1885. After the Ballot Act, 1872, these workers were less liable to pressure from employers and could use their vote as they thought fit [Chapter 7, Picture 48]. Randolph Churchill realised that these voters could be captured for a social-minded Conservative party. He urged the party boldly to come to terms with democracy:

> The Conservative party will never exercise power until it has gained the confidence of the working classes; and the working classes are quite determined to govern themselves, and will not be either driven or hoodwinked by any class or class interests. Our interests are perfectly safe if we trust them fully, frankly, and freely. . . . If you want to gain the confidence of the working classes let them have a share and a large share – a real share and not a sham share – in your party Councils and in your party government.

20 In contrast with the well fed and well clothed children of the skilled workers, were the thousands of poorly dressed and undernourished children of the unskilled and lowly paid.

But most working class voters tended to support the Liberal candidates with whom they felt more affinity in religion and philosophy; like their employers, the leaders of the working class believed in laissez faire, in self help, in rewards for the more sucessful [Picture 19]. Some local Liberal associations had the sense to adopt working men as their candidates in areas where the workers formed the bulk of the electorate.

Working class MPs

The Trade Union Congress had met for the first time in 1868. Its leaders realised that they would have to try and persuade Parliament to pass laws safeguarding the rights of trade unions and their members, and in 1869 a Labour Representation League was set up. In 1870 the League supported the attempt by George Odger to win an election in Southwark as an independent against both Liberal and Conservative candidates. This was unsuccessful but in 1874 the League succeeded in helping Thomas Burt and Alexander MacDonald – two ex-miners – to win Morpeth and Stafford, respectively. In these seats the Liberals had the good sense to withdraw their candidate, so that when Burt and MacDonald entered Parliament they sat with the other Liberals, took the Liberal Party whip and were, for all practical purposes, Liberal. By 1885 there were 11 such Lib–Lab MPs [Picture 22].

Militant Unionists

The 1880s were notable for the formation of a number of unions for lowly paid, unskilled workers. Annie Besant started a union for the girls working in Bryant and May's match factory; Will Thorne formed a union for the workers in the London Gasworks and, most important of all, Ben Tillett and Tom Mann helped to organise a union for the unskilled workers in the London Docks. Before 1880 such workers had been ignored by the well-paid, more or less fully employed skilled workmen who had high wages (of about £2 or £3 per week) and could afford the high fees charged by their unions. Out of these fees the unions of skilled workers paid benefits to their members whenever they were sick, unemployed, or retired. Such workers gained on the roundabouts of wages and the swings of welfare benefits. They enjoyed a high standard of living—their children being well-fed and well-dressed, their wives not having to go to work but being able to enjoy their role as homemakers.

The unskilled workers, on the other hand, were often out of work; even when employed they were poorly paid – at Bryant and May's they earned 2d an hour, in the London Docks only 4d per hour. For these men and their families life was grim [Picture 20]; these were the families who were the subjects of Rowntree's *Poverty: a study in Town Life* which showed that about one-third of the British people lived in desperate poverty, and of Jack London's novel, *The People of the Abyss*, which describes the dismal life led by some of these people.

Poorly housed, badly fed and clothed, frequently sick and off work, no one had thought they could be unionised. The 1880s proved that even such workers could form unions, could provide leaders to lead a strike against employers who could be forced to pay better wages. But even 6d an hour did not enable the London Docker to buy or rent a decent house [Picture 21]; nor did it help him to pay the insurance premiums to provide him with a pension or unemployment benefit. If his life and that of his family was to be improved he would need a whole series of Acts passed by a socially-minded Parliament. Neither the Conservative nor Liberal Parties seemed inclined to pass such laws.

Socialism

The idea that the State should become more involved in the social life of the country had been proposed by early trade union leaders such as Robert Owen

21 Low wages and frequent unemployment led to bad housing and high mortality rates for slum dwellers in London in 1889. Neither the Gladstone Liberals nor the Salisbury Tories did much to improve life for these people.

in the 1820s and by Chamberlain in the 1870s. [Chapter 3, Picture 15.] In the 1880s a wide variety of people began to advocate such activity, arguing that the richest country in the world could not afford to allow so many of its people to live in such poor conditions as were revealed by government and private inquiries. Clergymen such as the Rev. Andrew Mearns wanted a State pension as well as subsidised council housing; writers such as Bernard Shaw and H. G. Wells helped to form the Fabian Society which produced a series of pamphlets addressed to politicians, arguing that the State should look after the unemployed, the sick, the old and the poor. Henry George, an American, wrote a best-selling book *Poverty* which showed how taxation could be used to provide the funds to make life better for the less well-off. Robert Blatchford started a weekly newspaper *The Clarion* which spread the ideas of Henry George and the Fabians among the working classes.

Independent Labour

In 1888 Keir Hardie, a Scottish miners' leader, tried to get himself elected as the Liberal candidate at Lanark. He failed and so stood as the 'Labour and Home Rule' candidate and although he came bottom of the poll, formed the Scottish Labour Party. In the next few years a number of local Labour parties were formed in Yorkshire and Lancashire. At the general election of 1892 all five candidates of the Scottish Labour Party were defeated but Keir Hardie won West Ham and John Burns won Battersea South, while Ben Tillett just lost Bradford. It was at Bradford that in 1893 a conference was called to consider the formation of an Independendt Labour Party [Picture 22]. By 1895 this Party had 10,000 members, many of them members of other socialist societies (Ramsay MacDonald was a Fabian) or of a trade union (George Barnes was secretary of the Amalgamated Engineering Union). At successive conferences the TUC had been asked to approve the formation of a Labour Party which would be supported by the trade union movement. Each year the majority of delegates to the TUC had voted against such a motion, preferring its links with the Liberals. In 1899 the Amalgamated Society of Railway Servants submitted a resolution instructing the parliamentary committee

> to invite the cooperation of all the cooperative, socialistic, trade union and other working-class organizations to jointly cooperate on lines mutually agreed upon in convening a special congress of representatives from such of the above-named organizations as may be willing to take part to devise ways and means for securing the return of an increased number of Labour members to the next Parliament.

This resolution was only carried by 546,000 votes to 434,000, but it led to a meeting on 28 February 1900 at the Memorial Hall in Farringdon Street, London. Representatives of the Fabian Society, the Independent Labour Party, the Cooperative Society and the TUC decided to set up a Labour Representation Committee to which affiliated organisations were to pay ten shillings a year for every thousand members. The Committee was to have an executive of seven trade unionists, two representatives from the ILP and one from the Fabian Society.

Skilled workers and the Labour Party

The skilled workers had not felt the need for the Labour Party as had the unskilled workers. They had voted against the idea in 1899 and gave little support to the Party formed in 1900. These were the unions which had the money and the leaders to make the Party a viable force. They were driven into the Labour Party by the Taff Vale decision [Picture 23] which the Conservative government refused to alter by a new Trade Union Act. This made them realise that they, too,

35

22 Keir Hardie and his Independent Labour Party refused to join other working class MPs who sat with the Liberals.

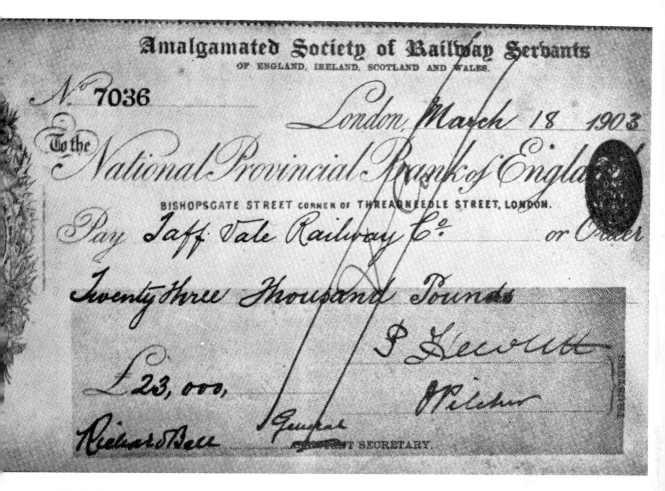

23 The Taff Vale cheque. The Company claimed damages from the Union after a strike. In addition, the Union had to pay £19,000 in legal costs. After this no union was anxious to use its strike weapon.

needed a voice in Parliament – and so they joined the Labour Party which increased its membership from 376,000 in 1901 to 861,000 in 1903. A political levy of 1d per week was collected from every member of a union affiliated to the Labour Party and this provided a fund out of which the Party could pay MPs £200 a year as well as provide the money to fight elections in hundreds of constituencies.

The Liberal and Labour Parties

Ramsay MacDonald became secretary of the new Party in 1900. He realised that the infant Party would not win many seats if it tried to fight against both Liberal and Conservative candidates. He realised also that his Labour Party and the Liberal parties shared a number of ideas in common; they were both opposed to the Tariff Reform policy of Joseph Chamberlain which was tearing the Conservatives apart [Chapter 5, Picture 28]; they both opposed the 1902 Education Act and both wanted to do more for the less well-off members of society. MacDonald and the Liberal Chief Whip, Herbert Gladstone, made an electoral pact by which each agreed to withdraw candidates in certain constituencies to leave the other party a free hand against the Conservative candidate. This was one of the reasons for the massive defeat suffered by the Conservatives in the 1906 election. It was also one of the reasons for the election of 53 Labour MPs to Parliament. Balfour, the leader of the defeated Conservatives, wrote:

> We have here to do with something much more important than the swing of the pendulum or all the squabbles about free trade and fiscal reform. We are face to face (no doubt in a milder form) with the socialist difficulties which loom so large on the continent. Unless I am greatly mistaken, the election of 1906 inaugurates a new era.

The War 1914–1918 and the Parties

Many Labour supporters had become disillusioned with their Party by 1914. What had it achieved by playing at politics? Many militant union leaders believed that more would be achieved by strike action against employers rather than waiting for the slower process of persuading Parliament to raise living standards. During the War the Labour Party was badly split between those who opposed the War and those who supported the British entry into it. Leaders like MacDonald and Snowden became unpopular as pacifists while others such as Barnes and Henderson entered Lloyd George's Cabinet in 1916.

However, as we shall see (Chapter 5), the War broke the Liberal Party so that there was a vacuum which the Labour Party was able to fill. The war also made many millions of people turn against the leaders who had taken Britain into a costly and murderous war and so made them likely converts for the Party, some of whose leaders had opposed the war. They were also likely converts to a Party which promised to build a better world – particularly as Lloyd George and his Coalition government showed no signs of being able to live up to their slogan of building a country 'Fit for Heroes'.

In 1918 the Party adopted a new constitution, Clause 4 of which promised the nationalisation of all the means of production, distribution and exchange. As well as allowing trade unions and other societies to become affiliated members of the Labour Party, the 1918 constitution set up Labour Party Associations in each constituency – which reduced the number of people still willing to join the Independent Labour Party which continued to exist as an affiliated society but slowly died. The constituency associations tended to be dominated by militant socialists, but the Party leaders relied on the votes of the large trade unions at the

THE LABOUR BIRD
AND THE
LIBERAL WORM.

24 The Liberals supported the Labour Government in 1924 and so became even less of an alternative to the Conservatives, while the Labour Party became increasingly confident, better known, and more widely supported.

Party's Annual Conferences to squash the more radical motions proposed by the socialists. [Chapter 6, Picture 42]

The Party constitution declared that the Parliamentary Labour Party was subject to the decisions of the Party's Annual Conference – something which Chamberlain and Churchill had tried to insist on in the older parties in the nineteenth century. However, the leaders of the parliamentary Labour Party have usually made up their own minds and often acted against the wishes of the Annual Conference. Sometimes this has led to serious disputes. In the 1960s Conference decisions on nuclear disarmament were deliberately opposed by the Party leader, Hugh Gaitskell, and the Party was threatened with disruption.

The Party and the Militants

The Labour Party grew in power as the Liberal Party declined and in the 1922 election the Labour Party emerged as the official Opposition. In the 1923 [Chapter 5, Picture 34] election the Conservatives won 218 seats, Labour 191 seats and Liberals 158 seats. Baldwin, the Conservative leader, refused to take office and advised King George V to send for MacDonald, who became the first Labour Prime Minister.

However, his government, partly because it was dependent on the Liberals for power [Picture 24], partly because it was made of men with little experience, proved incapable of dealing with the problem of unemployment. This led militant trade unionists to decide that direct strike action was a better weapon than the political one: hence the General Strike of 1926. The failure of this Strike led to a return to the political weapon and the return of a second Labour government in 1929. Unfortunately MacDonald and his government were faced with the worst economic depression the world had ever known. MacDonald hoped that it would be easier to deal with this problem by forming a Coalition government. This led to a split in the Labour Party – most of the leaders supporting MacDonald while the rank and file regarded him as a traitor who had betrayed the best interests of the Party. [Picture 25]

Post-War Power

Although the Party regained many seats in the Election of 1935, it was the Second World War 1939–45 which brought it back to power.

The Attlee government nationalised many of the country's major industries, passed a series of Acts which established the Welfare State which we have today and by 1949 had so changed the social life of the country that even Conservative leaders spoke about 'a social revolution' [Picture 26]. However, the fact that the government nationalised some and not all industry meant that it had moved away from the ideals proposed in Clause 4 of the constitution: the fact that the

25 The Coalition Government formed by Ramsay MacDonald in 1931. *(Seated: left to right)* Snowden, Baldwin, MacDonald, Samuels, Sankey. *(Standing: left to right)* Cunliffe-Lister, Thomas, Reading, Chamberlain, Hoare.

government helped private industry to recover from the War meant that it accepted a 'mixed economy', in which there would be some nationalised, socialist industry and some private industry. Equally, the government, while proposing a minimum standard of living for the old, sick and unemployed, did very little to prevent the rich from enjoying a very high standard of living. As well as accepting a mixed economy, the Party was also accepting the mixed social life. This was a far cry from the talk of equality on which the Party had been founded. But most of its members were quite happy in 1950 and 1951 to vote for a Party which had shown itself capable of producing great leaders such as Ernest Bevin and

26 Sir William Beveridge's Report (1942) called for a high increase in government spending as part of the creation of a better Britain. The Labour Party took Britain down this road after 1945.

Aneurin Bevan, great Acts such as the National Health Service, and great changes so that nearly everyone had a job and the foundations were laid for great new industries which would produce the wealth for the affluent society of the 1950s. Like the Party leaders, the majority of the party's supporters were more interested in results than in theory, more interested in houses than ideas.

5 Decline of the Liberals

Liberal Principles

When Gladstone was campaigning in the 1860s and 1870s [Chapter 3, Picture 14], he continually told his audience that the Liberal Party stood for 'Peace, Retrenchment and Reform'. In supporting a policy of 'Peace' the Liberal Party marked itself off from Disraeli's Tories who were prepared for a more adventurous and vigorous foreign and imperial policy. Gladstone preferred to withdraw the British from the Transvaal; the Tories before and after him occupied it. He preferred to submit the American claim over the Alabama incident to an international tribunal, rather than risk the danger of a war with the USA. He opposed Disraeli's annexation policies in both Egypt and Afghanistan.

Gladstone [Picture 27] and the Liberals believed in a peaceful policy because the opposite – a warlike policy – would cost money and so lead to increased

27 The Anglican leader of the mainly Nonconformist Liberals making his last speech in the Commons, 1894. On the Opposition bench can be seen Balfour (centre) and Chamberlain (extreme left).

taxation. The second main Liberal principle was 'Retrenchment', which meant that the government would not spend more of the taxpayers' money than was absolutely essential. This meant that in addition to having a peaceful foreign policy, Gladstone and the Liberals were not prepared to support Chamberlain's ideas on social reform [Chapter 3, Picture 15] – such as pensions, help for the unemployed and homeless – because these would all have meant an increase in the level of taxation.

The third Liberal principle was 'Reform' by which Gladstone meant that existing institutions – such as the Army, the Civil Service or the Universities – should be reformed so that they were more efficient (and less costly) and so that there was equal freedom of entry and promotion to members of all classes and religions.

Out of power 1886–1906

Gladstone resigned after the Liberal Party had been split by Chamberlain (Chapter 3) and apart from a brief period of government from 1892 to 1894 the Liberals were out of power for the next twenty years. The electorate preferred to support a Conservative party which was not prepared to give Home Rule to Ireland but, on the contrary, was prepared to increase the size of the British Empire. Under Lord Salisbury's leadership the Conservatives became the favourites of the electorate, particularly after Joe Chamberlain joined the Conservative Party.

In 1901 the Conservatives won a resounding election success while the people were rejoicing over the British army's successes against the Boers in South Africa. However, by 1905 the political picture had changed. The Liberals, split over whether they should support or oppose the government's action against the Boers, were united by the Conservative decision to force ratepayers to spend money on supporting Catholic and Anglican schools. 'Rome on the Rates' was a slogan used by Liberal candidates to rouse the religious fears of the Noncon-formists. The Nonconformist conscience was also roused by stories of 'Chinese slavery' in British mines in South Africa. Chinese labourers were recruited to work in the South African mines and had to sign an indenture by which they promised not to leave their employer for a number of years, while he laid down the amount paid in wages. This was translated into 'slavery'.

The trade unions were roused against the Conservatives by the Taff Vale decision [Chapter 4, Picture 23], and the government's refusal to do anything about this; the Liberals, on the other hand, promised that if they came to power they would bring in a new law which would safeguard the unions' 'right to strike' without danger to their funds. But above all else the Liberals were roused by the Tariff Reform campaign of Joseph Chamberlain [Picture 28]. Ever since 1846 Britain had been more or less a Free Trade country paying almost no taxes on imports in the country. This meant that food and raw material came in

44

PAPA COBDEN TAKING MASTER ROBERT A FREE TRADE WALK.

HISTORY REVERSES ITSELF;

28 Joseph Chamberlain tried to force his leader, Balfour, to abandon Free Trade. He was less successful than Cobden had been in 1846 when he had persuaded Peel to adopt Free Trade.

without paying import duties; the cost of living was therefore lower than it would have been if there were such import duties. But in the last years of the nineteenth century many foreign countries had been sending in increasing quantities of manufactured goods to compete with home produced goods in the British market – so that there was an ever-increasing level of unemployment, while manufacturers' profits fell. Britain's exporters, on the other hand, found that when they tried to sell in foreign countries they had to pay import duties which increased the price of the British imports and so made them more difficult to sell. This again led to a fall in the demand for British goods and so to unemployment [Picture 29].

CAUGHT NAPPING!

29 German industry was capturing an increasing share of Britain's trade after 1880. Governments did nothing to stop this.

30 Prime Minister Asquith led the government which brought in many social reforms (1908–16). Many people believed that the Liberals were being forced to adopt these new policies because of fear of the growing Labour Party with its socialist policies.

Chamberlain proposed that the government should impose tariffs on foreign imports into this country, and that these should include a tariff on food. He hoped to persuade the countries of the Empire to put a lower tariff on British goods than on goods from other countries. In return, Britain would put a lower tariff on food imports from Empire countries than on food from other overseas countries. This would help both Britain and the Empire, and might create a more united Empire.

This suggestion allowed the Liberals to argue that Chamberlain was turning his back on fifty years of British history. The Labour Party also believed in Free Trade and this lay behind the electoral pact with the Liberals, made in 1903 (Chapter 4).

New Liberalism

When the Liberals won their major victory in 1906, Lloyd George began to talk about a New Liberalism which would differ from Gladstonian Liberalism. Instead of 'Retrenchment' the new Liberals would spend the rich taxpayers' money to help the poor, the old and the sick. For many people this change had come too late – they had already joined or supported the Labour Party which was pledged to go further and faster than Lloyd George. For other voters, however, this was too much and too soon, and this led many of the rich to leave the Liberal Party and to join the Conservatives [Picture30]. In particular, it was a major reason for the House of Lords becoming a predominantly Conservative House whereas in the past it had been less so.

New Liberals

Lloyd George [Picture 33] and Winston Churchill were the leaders of the New Liberals and they frequently quarrelled with the older Liberals who did not see the need for the change of policy. The Liberal Government of 1906–14 was an uneasy alliance between the old and the new. It is possible that the strains of normal political life would have been sufficient to have split this Party.

The War 1914–18

The strains of war proved more than this uneasy Party could bear. In the first place the leader, Asquith, proved incapable or unwilling to act as though the war was all important; he refused to bring in conscription, preferring to leave men free to volunteer for the Services. Even when the volunteer system proved unable to bring in all the men required by the Service Chiefs, Asquith was unwilling to change his policies. Liberalism meant freedom, conscription meant force and Asquith would not change. Similarly, he was unwilling to compel industrialists to produce the weapons and materials necessary for the prosecution

31 Lloyd George increased taxation in his 1908 budget. To many people this increase seemed like a murderous attack on the rich – who supported the Conservative Party.

32 Many Liberal ideas died during the war when governments played an ever-increasing part in people's lives.

of the war. He preferred to leave them free to produce whatever they wanted to.

By 1916 his failure was evident and the leading politicians in other parties were prepared to support Lloyd George as Prime Minister in place of Asquith. Many Liberals, supporters of Asquith, thought that for Lloyd George to accept the support of the Conservatives was almost treachery to his Liberal past: they continued to support Asquith. Other Liberals, realising the need for a more dynamic leadership if the war was to be won, swallowed their Liberal pride and joined the Coalition government. [Picture 34]

By 1918 most Liberal ideas had been thrown overboard: the government interfered in almost every walk of people's lives, telling industrialists what they were to do, rationing food, providing money for the old and injured as well as the families of men in the services. By 1918 a whole new administrative machine had been created – to help win the war, but it was a machine which was the very opposite of what Gladstone had meant by Retrenchment and Reform.

By 1918 also the British people had suffered a great deal – and in return wanted a better country once the war was over. For most ordinary people this meant a country in which there were better homes, more schools, more doctors, more jobs – and they expected the government to play a part in providing these things. This was a 'socialism' which was foreign to Liberalism. Men who wanted these changes tended to switch their support from the Liberal to the Labour Parties.

Elections 1918–24

The signs of the Liberals' decline could be seen in the election results of 1918–24. [Picture 34] Lloyd George led his Coalition government of Conservatives and Liberals into the 1918 election against Liberal and Labour candidates. Not surprisingly his popularity – as the man who had won the war – was enough to help his candidates to win many seats. The Labour Party, unpopular for having opposed the war, did better than it could have expected but the Liberals, led by Asquith, did badly, even Asquith losing his seat.

33 Lloyd George resigned in 1922 after the Conservative MPs decided not to support his Coalition Government. In 1924 he campaigned as leader of his own Liberal Party. Many older voters still thought of him as a Radical. Younger voters had already turned to the Labour Party as the radical alternative to the Conservatives.

By 1922 the Conservatives in the Coalition had grown tired of Lloyd George and they forced him to resign to make way for a Conservative Prime Minister, Bonar Law. In 1923 Bonar Law had to retire and Stanley Baldwin became Prime Minister. In the 1923 election the two wings of the Liberal Party made an uneasy alliance, but the Labour Party became the second largest Party in the Commons, claiming the right to speak as the official Opposition and being the Party which the King sent for when Baldwin refused to try to form a government in 1924.

The Liberals and voting habits

One of the features of British elections is that very few people change their voting habits throughout their lives; if they vote Liberal at their first-ever election then about 80 per cent of them are likely to vote Liberal at every subsequent election. It was obvious from the results of 1918–24 that many new voters (coming of age in time for the election) were voting for the Labour or Conservative Parties. This meant that the Liberal voters tended to be older people carrying on a habit of pre-war voting. In time these would die – and the Liberal Party's chances would die with them.

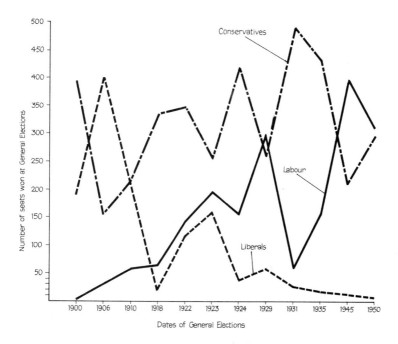

34   The continued decline of the Liberal Party. A graph showing the number of seats won by each of the three main parties between 1900 and 1950. In the elections of 1918 and 1931 the Conservatives were part of a Coalition which won huge victories over the Opposition. The graph shows how the Labour Party has replaced the Liberal Party as the alternative to the Conservatives.

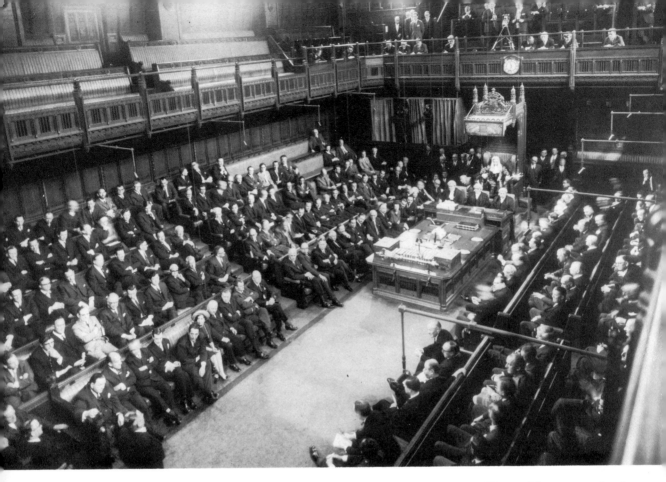

35 The state opening of Parliament 1966. It is easy to see how the House of Commons makes for a two-party system where the two sides sit facing each other.

Another feature of our voting habits is that about 75 per cent of us tend to follow our parents' voting pattern; if we are brought up in a house where the parents vote Conservative it is likely that we too will vote Conservative. As fewer and fewer parents tended to vote Liberal in the 1920s, so the likelihood was that the Liberals would get an ever-decreasing number of votes in the 1950s, when the children of the 1920 voters came of age.

Finally, there is the question of the two-party system. The British House of Commons tends to make for a two party system – one party sits on one side of the House and the other party sits opposite, [Picture 35]. In a semi-circular House (as in France or Italy), there is room for a larger number of parties since the difference between a Member and his neighbour is not so clearly marked as it is in in Britain, where an MP has to cross the floor of the House and change sides if he wants to vote against his Party. Since there is a tendency to a two-Party system this means that there is room for only one Party of change – the Conservatives by definition being against many changes. This Party of change could have been *either* the Labour *or* the Liberal Parties. *Both* could not exist. As the Labour Party grew so the Liberal Party had to decline.

36 Honor Blackman, TV and film star, was one of the younger voters who supported the Liberal Party in the 1966 election.

Modern Liberals

In the 1950s and 1960s many young people had become discontented with the records of both the Labour and the Conservative governments. They have therefore tended to join the Liberal Party which now and again in the 1960s seemed likely to replace the Labour Party as the main party of the Left. Young candidates, well known personalities of stage and television became candidates for this new, younger Liberal Party [Picture 36]. But they found it difficult to alter the voting habits of the majority of the electorate, who still vote for the Labour or the Conservative Parties – or, if fed up with both, may not vote at all. Furthermore, the Liberals suffer from lack of money; the Conservatives get their money from big companies, from rich patrons and from industrial organisations: the Labour Party gets its money from the Trade Unions. The Liberals have no such guaranteed source. They have found it difficult to get enough money to pay for election campaigns – for posters, advertisements in the press, the hiring of halls and the paying of speakers' expenses. There seems little likelihood that they can overcome this major obstacle to electoral success.

6 Party Organisation

Constituencies

There are various ways in which the country may be divided up – for cricket we divide the country into counties, for local government we have metropolitan, county and urban divisions. For political purposes the country is divided into constituencies, each containing on average about 75,000 voters. As some areas of our older towns are redeveloped so that the population falls, so the boundaries of the constituencies have to be re-drawn and for this purpose a Boundaries Commission has been set up to recommend necessary changes to the government.

37 A map of the constituencies electing MPs in 1832.

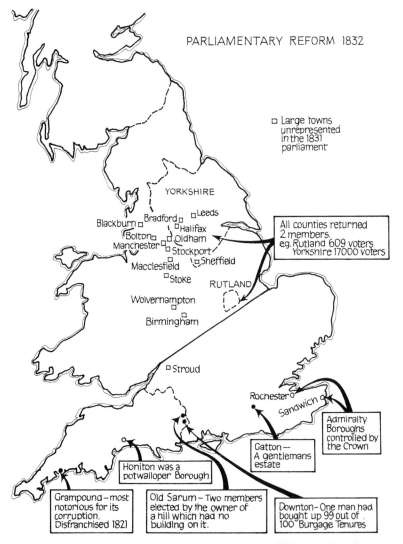

PARLIAMENTARY REFORM 1832

□ Large towns unrepresented in the 1831 parliament

YORKSHIRE

□Leeds
Bradford□
Blackburn□
□Halifax
Bolton□ □Oldham
Manchester□
□Stockport
Macclesfield□ □Sheffield
□Stoke

RUTLAND

Wolverhampton□

Birmingham□

All counties returned 2 members. e.g. Rutland 609 voters Yorkshire 17000 voters

□ Stroud

Rochester○
Sandwich○

Admiralty Boroughs controlled by the Crown

Gatton – A gentlemans estate

Honiton was a potwalloper Borough

Grampound – most notorious for its corruption. Disfranchised 1821

Old Sarum – Two members elected by the owner of a hill which had no building on it.

Downton – One man had bought up 99 out of 100 Burgage Tenures

38 The Labour Committee Rooms in the Putney Constituency. On the back wall is the map showing the constituency divided into wards, in each of which there will be a number of Polling Places (left wall).

Each constituency is divided into a number of wards [Picture 38], the boundaries of the wards being fixed by the Ministry of Local Government, and for party political purposes the electoral ward is the basis for membership and activity. An elector may become a member of the local Labour or Conservative Association which will allow him to attend the meetings of his Ward Association, to take part in the election of the officers of his Ward Association and the choosing of delegates to the Constituency Management Committee or Central Council. This in turn will choose a smaller Executive Committee which will be responsible for running the affairs of the local Party.

The Party Member
Although a Party may persuade many thousands of people to support its candidate at a General Election, very few of these supporters actually join a political party. Few people feel sufficiently deeply about politics to get involved in monthly meetings of a Ward group – so that only five or six may go to such meetings. Very few people feel that they want to have a hand in the choosing of

55

delegates to a Party National Conference, or the writing of resolutions to be submitted to the Town Council, the Government or the Party Headquarters. Most people feel that they would prefer to leave such matters to the few who are more politically educated and willing to be involved.

Above all, few people want to give up their time to do the work that is asked of a Party Member, who will be expected to take an active part at election times. [Picture 39]

Choosing the Candidate

One of the main functions of the active Party member is to take a part in the choosing of the Party's candidate for an election. Each Ward Association and each affiliated organisation (such as a trade union in the case of the Labour Party) is allowed to put forward the name of a potential candidate. In most cases the names chosen will be taken from a list supplied by the Party's Headquarters – most potential candidates having previously submitted their names to the Party for vetting. The Party Headquarters list shows how long the person has been a member of the Party, what offices – if any – he has held inside the Party, what his occupation and interests are.

39 The active Party members, who are the voluntary workers, run the election campaign.

The Ward Associations do not have to choose someone from this list; they may nominate someone local who they believe would make a good candidate. In this case the Constituency Officers submit this 'outsider's' case before the National Officers who may or may not decide to recommend that this new name be added to the Party's list of candidates.

There are several sorts of people who find it difficult to get themselves nominated as potential candidates. Most local Associations are reluctant to nominate women, so that although over half the electors are women, only about one-twentieth of the MPs are female, while few women become Cabinet Ministers. Working class men find it almost impossible to be selected as Conservative candidates while even inside the Labour Party there is an increasing tendency to support candidates who have been to University, so that there is a declining number of trade union and working class MPs inside the Labour Party.

The Constituency Party Executive Committee may receive as many as a hundred names when they invite nominations for consideration as a candidate. Their first job is to draw up a list of applicants and to decide which of these should be deleted. Then they draw up a short list of five or six candidates and these are

40 Selecting the prospective Conservative candidate for the Arundel and Shoreham constituency in February, 1971. Three Conservative applicants with their wives had to appear before a selection conference. Left to right are Mrs and Mr Douglas Hurd (later a Civil Servant in Number 10 Downing Street); Mrs and Mr John Stanley; Mrs and Mr Richard Luce – the successful candidate. The conference lasted three hours during which time the constituency meeting was picketed by angry member of the Womens' Liberation Movement, who objected to the candidates' wives being used as arguments for and against their husbands' applications.

41 Herbert Morrison (centre) waving to the crowd of supporters after winning the safe Labour seat at Hackney in 1935.

usually invited to meet the larger Constituency Management Committee. The method of selection may vary from place to place but in general each candidate will be asked to make a short speech and to answer questions from the Committee who will then decide which of the short-listed candidates should be the Party's candidate at the next election.

In some constituencies the choice of the Committee is almost guaranteed election to Parliament; in Ebbw Vale the Labour candidate is almost sure to win – and by a huge majority over his Conservative rival. Equally the Conservative candidate in Arundel is almost guaranteed to beat his Labour rival. This means that in some constituencies the small Management Committee is really choosing not a candidate but an MP [Picture 40]. If an MP offends the members of this Committee they are able to unseat him by choosing a new candidate at the time of the next election – in Bournemouth, Nigel Nicolson was unseated by his own Party Management Committee because he had spoken and voted against the Conservative Government's Suez policy in 1956. Similarly, Labour 'rebel' MPs have found themselves unseated. However, there are examples of a rebel refusing to accept the decision of the Committee. S. O. Davies had been the Labour MP for Merthyr for many years when, in 1970, the Management Committee decided that he was too old and should be replaced by another, younger, candidate. S. O. Davies decided to fight the 1970 election as an Independent and showed that personal popularity with the electorate as a whole was greater than his popularity with the Management Committee: he won the seat.

Social functions

The ward and the constituency parties try to provide more than merely political activities for their members; there are coffee mornings, whist drives, summer fairs, garden fetes, jumble sales and annual dinners, all intended to bring the active workers together in a social function [Picture 42]. Another purpose of such functions is to raise money required by the local party to help it pay the rent on local headquarters, the salary of the full-time party agent and to send in money to the National Headquarters. In addition, the local party will have to pay for posters, pamphlets and speakers' expenses during election times and between elections.

42 The Labour Party's Annual Conference, 1963. A high spot of each Party's year is the annual conference, when delegates from local and affiliated Associations get a chance to meet, to speak, and to see the Party leaders.

43 Labour Party's
Headquarters, London.

Party Headquarters

Not very far from the House of Parliament is Smith Square, in one corner of
which the Conservative Party has its National headquarters while across the
other side of the Square is Transport House, the headquarters of the Labour
Party [Picture 43]. The casual observer might think that each of the leading
parties was keeping an eye on the other. In these headquarters work a number
of paid, full-time officers and workers. They write the pamphlets which candidates
use at election time; they do research for candidates and MPs who want to be
better informed on a certain subject; they prepare material for issue to the Press.

All of this, of course, costs a good deal of money and as we have seen (Chapter 5)
the Labour and Conservative Parties have large sums of money from various
sources. The Liberal Party, on the other hand, suffers in not having the sort of
income which the two larger parties enjoy.

7 Electioneering

Date of Elections

The Parliament Act of 1911 laid down that a General Election must be held at least every five years. In fact, very few governments have stuck to that timing. During the two World Wars, for example, it was felt that it was not right to disrupt the war effort by holding an election. The Parliament elected in 1910 remained in being until the General Election of 1918, while the 1935 Parliament remained in being until the Germans had been defeated in 1945. Even in peace time, however, few Parliaments have remained for their full five years: we had eight General Elections between 1945 and 1970.

The right to call for a General Election is one of the powers enjoyed by the Prime Minister (Chapter 9). He can ask the Monarch to announce that Parliament is to be dissolved and an election is to be held whenever he wishes. Prime Ministers have always used this power to call an election for a date which they think will suit the interests of their own Party; they would not call for an election when the government was obviously unpopular or doing badly. On the other hand, if there were signs that the economy was in a very healthy state, with most people having a job, and the government's policy seemed to be popular, then a Prime Minister might call for an election, even though he might have been in office for only a short time. Harold Wilson was Prime Minister after the election in October 1964 but had only a very small majority in the Commons – the electorate in 1964 had obviously not made up their minds whether to trust the Labour Party. When there were signs that his government was more popular, Mr Wilson called another election for March 1966 (not two years after the previous one) and the Labour Party had a majority of over 100. He had obviously picked the right time for the election.

In theory a Prime Minister could ask for an election to be held at any time during the year. In practice, however, his freedom is somewhat limited. Few voters would welcome the idea of an election on, say, Boxing Day – when they were still recovering from the Christmas party. The Party's active workers who have to do all the hard work during an election wouldn't welcome one in February or November, when they are likely to be cold and wet as they tramp from door to door [Picture 44]. Equally they wouldn't like to give up their summer holidays in July or August to go to work on the electorate, which might, anyhow, be away from home and unable to vote. This means that a Prime Minister usually calls an election for June or October – before the summer holidays have started and before winter has set in.

The tradition has grown up that elections should be held on Thursdays and

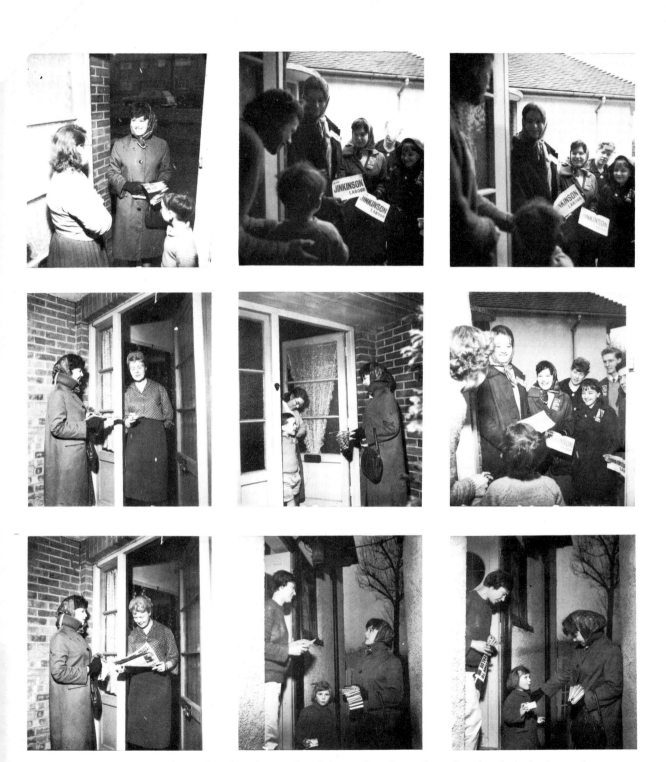

44 Canvassing from door to door is better done in good weather than in bad – hence there are few General Elections called during the winter.

45 The candidates tour their constituencies, addressing meetings in school halls, market squares, village greens – wherever they can gather a crowd. This is Mr Attlee speaking in the 1950 Election, one of the few called in wintertime.

political writers in newspapers and commentators on TV enjoy explaining to people why the date of the election must be 'one of the following six Thursdays' which may make them appear fairly learned prophets, whereas in fact they are merely using their knowledge of the political system.

Canvassing

When Parliament is dissolved there are no MPs, although the Ministers continue in office as the government has to be carried on. Who, for example, would take action if the country were invaded and there was no government? The former MP is usually adopted as his Party's candidate for the next election – although, as we have seen (Chapter 6) there are cases of 'rebel' MPs being replaced by their local Association. The Opposition Parties will have already chosen their candidates and all of them will have spent some time in making themselves known to the local Party members [Picture 45]. They will have addressed ward and local Party meetings, attended fetes and whist drives, opened bazaars and written to the local newspapers, all to get themselves known to the local Party workers.

46 Modern technology comes to the candidate's aid. A loudspeaker van in a motorcade is now an almost essential part of a campaign.

Clearly it is on the local Party worker that the candidate depends. Every day after Parliament has been dissolved, groups of Party workers will be busy for many hours every day. Some will be addressing envelopes to every voter in the constituency; others will be putting election propaganda into the envelopes, while still others will be tramping around the constituency, pushing this material into letter-boxes. Someone will be getting together a list of Party supporters who will be willing to have posters in their windows; others will be seeing to the printing and distribution of the posters; someone will have a list of supporters willing to spend polling day driving their cars to and from the polling booths, carrying voters who otherwise might not be able to get to the poll. [Picture 46]

A large number of Party workers will spend every evening for three weeks or so going to every house in the constituency, trying to find out which voters are likely to vote for and which will probably vote against the Party. By ticking off the likely support promised to their Party, a constituency has a rough idea of whether or not they have a chance of winning the election. They also know from the questions asked at the door what sort of things are worrying the voters, and perhaps this will help the candidate and other speakers to prepare their material for their public speeches. [Picture 45]

The vote
We have seen (Chapter 5) that there is good evidence for believing that very few people change their voting habits throughout their lifetime; if a person votes Labour at his very first election, then there is an 80 per cent chance that he will continue to do so in every following election. However, this still means that something like one voter in every five is likely to change his mind and vote for another Party at a following election. This is one reason for canvassing and propaganda – the Parties hope to catch this 'floating voter'.

Then again there are millions of people who have never voted before but come of age between elections. A person aged 13 in 1970 did not vote in the 1970 General Election. But in any election held after 1975 this former schoolchild will have the right to vote. This is another reason for all the activity at election time – the Parties are trying to win the support of the 'first voter' knowing, as we have seen, that this probably means a life-long supporter.

In the nineteenth century there was good evidence that the voter gave his support to a particular candidate; the slogan 'Vote for Bloggs' meant a good deal if the voters knew and trusted Bloggs. But there is plenty of evidence to show that in recent years the candidate is not a very important factor in deciding how the election will go. Most writers estimate that no candidate is worth more than about 500 votes – so that whether Bloggs or Cloggs is the candidate doesn't make a great deal of difference.

Today, it seems, the voters support or oppose a Party and not a particular candidate. They will know about the Party's policies – from newspaper com-

47 The Returning Officer is in charge of the organisation of the election and he has to make the official declaration of the result after the counting has finished. Here, Clement Attlee, successful in 1950, is thanking the Returning Officer (on his left) for the hard work done by his staff.

ments, from interviews on TV and radio, from the speeches of prominent members of the Party, and in the case of the former government they will know what that Party has done recently.

But if the candidates can take small comfort from the fact that few electors bother about them, the Parties can also take little comfort from the evidence that few electors vote for a particular Party. Some do, of course – the active Party workers, the lifelong committed voters. But the new voters and the floating voters are much more likely to be voting *against* the Government or the Opposition rather than voting *for* something [Chapter 8, Picture 59]. All the evidence indicates that people are less interested in what a party proposes than in what the other Party has either failed to do or has failed to promise. This is why so much electioneering is concerned with attacking the other side. The voter has to be persuaded that the other side is no good, should be voted against.

Finally, there is increasing evidence that the voters are swayed by the quality of the Party Leaders. Perhaps this was always so – certainly the influence of Gladstone and Disraeli was very great. But in modern elections, when the Party leaders appear so frequently on TV and radio, on posters and pamphlets, it is even more important that they should be men whom the voters will support.

Voting day

In every constituency there is an electoral register which shows the names and addresses of everyone entitled to vote at the election and gives every voter a number. The local Returning Officer (usually the Mayor) will have named a number of places as Polling Stations.

Each Polling Station has to be prepared with a number of booths where the voter can go to mark his paper in secret, with boxes into which he can put his folded marked paper, and with a staff who will give out the ballot papers, mark off the voter's name from the Electoral Register – to make sure that no one tries to vote more than once. [Picture 48]

The Parties are also concerned about the Polling Stations. Each Party will try to have someone on duty outside the station to collect the names and voting numbers of those who have voted. This information is taken back to the Party's Committee rooms, where a copy of the Electoral Register is used to mark off the names of likely supporters who have voted. This then gives other Party workers a chance to go to the houses of supporters who haven't voted, and to remind them of their promise to vote and, if necessary, to offer to take them by car to the Polling Station. [Picture 49]

When the Polling Stations close at 9.00 p.m. the ballot boxes are sealed by the Returning Officer's staff and taken by car to the Counting Centre – usually the Town Hall. When all the boxes have been received they are opened and first of all the papers are counted to make sure that the totals agree with the totals already provided of the numbers of papers given out; this prevents anyone throwing in a number of pre-marked papers, or of taking out the papers from a Station where he thinks his Party might have done badly. [Picture 51]

When the totals are agreed, the ballot papers are then spread on tables in front of counters; these are usually members of the Town Council staff. They make bundles of the ballot papers marked in favour of 'Bloggs' on one side and bundles of those marked for his opponents on the other side. After this division the counters then put the papers in bundles of ten or twenty, turning up the top paper to show the successful candidate's name. Then these smaller bundles are put together into hundreds and so, finally, all papers are counted and a total agreed. [Picture 51]

The Parties will have supplied supporters to stand behind each counter to ensure that none of 'Blogg's' papers are put into 'Clogg's' pile – by accident or design. All the while the Returning Officer and the candidates are waiting in the Hall for the result to be brought to them. If a candidate sees the piles of votes massing up he may get an idea of how well or badly he has done. The result may be obvious long before the count has finished. In some constituencies the successful candidate gets only three votes more than his opponent. In these cases the loser will usually ask that the votes be re-counted – and there are many examples of the second count giving a different result to the first one. In some constituencies there may have to be a number of re-counts before the Parties agree on a result.

48 The Secret Ballot was first used in the Taunton By-Election in October 1873. This series of drawings was made to help the voters to understand the changes in the law.

49 Voluntary Party workers collecting the names and voting numbers of Chelsea Pensioners at the Polling Station.

50 Ballot boxes arriving at Lewisham Town Hall for the Count.

51 Voluntary Party workers (on the right) watch the Returning Officer's staff counting the votes.

The declaration

While the counting is going on in the Hall the active party workers will be waiting outside to hear the result. As soon as the Returning Officer is satisfied that a true result has been obtained he announces the result to the waiting crowd – and nowadays to the TV cameras.

The final result

When a constituency votes, it elects an MP to represent it in Parliament. When all the results from all the constituencies are in, then one or other Party will be seen to have a larger number of MP supporters than the other Parties. The Monarch will then send for the leader of that Party, and ask him to form a government.

Nowadays we do not have to wait very long before we know who is going to lead the new government. Once upon a time elections were spread over forty days, so that a defeated candidate could rush to another constituency and try his luck there – at the same election. In those days the people had to wait for six or seven weeks before they knew who was going to be the next Prime Minister. Today it is all over in one day. Because people tend to vote for or against a Party and not a particular candidate, and because people in one part of the country tend to behave like people in most other parts, we can now make a good guess at the result of the election once we have got the first two or three results. The first results come in at about 10.30 p.m. If these first results show, for example, that Labour voters are voting in high numbers (as in 1966) then we can reckon that every subsequent result will show roughly the same trend. By working out how many more Labour voters turned out in 1966 than in 1964, commentators could work out which seats the Conservatives might lose and so estimate the final result. Equally, once it was clear that Labour supporters were not turning out in the 1970 election, then the Conservative victory was obvious after only three or four results had been announced.

52   In the more leisurely 18th century, elections went on for a number of days. This view of Tonbridge during an election shows the banners, the band and the open polling station.

8 The Voter

Today's voter

Today almost everyone over the age of eighteen is entitled to vote at an election. The exceptions are few: only members of the House of Lords, prisoners and lunatics are not entitled to vote. We know that, owing to the work of the Boundaries Commission, most constituencies contain about 75,000 voters so that a vote in one constituency is worth roughly the same as a vote in another.

Former constituencies

Up to 1832 there were three types of constituency – the *Universities* of Oxford and Cambridge returned their own MPs, elected by graduates of those Universities. Each *County*, regardless of size, returned two MPs so that the 15,000 Yorkshire voters had the same value as the 600 Rutland voters [Chapter 6, Picture 37]. Then there were the *Boroughs*. These varied in type; some were known as *pot walloper* boroughs, because the vote was given to every householder who could show that he had a fireplace capable of boiling a pot. Others were *scot and lot* boroughs where every ratepayer was allowed to vote. There were *freemen* boroughs where only the few people who had been awarded the freedom of the borough could vote, and *corporation* boroughs where only the members of the town council could vote. A large number were *rotten* boroughs, where only a small number of people were allowed to vote.

This is a far cry from our universal system. If a 'pot walloper' left his borough to go and live in a 'freemen' borough he also lost the right to vote while, on the other hand, a non-voter in a 'corporation' borough could gain a vote if he moved to a 'scot and lot' borough and became a ratepayer. There were even one or two places such as Westminster [Picture 53] which allowed every man who had spent the previous night in the borough to have a vote.

Former voters

In the county elections every man who owned the freehold of land worth forty shillings a year had the right to vote. This at least was a uniform practice throughout the whole country, and meant that the voter was less likely to be open to a landowner's persuasion than if he were merely a tenant. However, it did mean that very wealthy (and possibly very independent-minded) men who only rented farms and estates did not have the right to vote – although their estates might have been much larger than that of a forty shilling freeholder. This was

53 Westminster was one of the few constituencies with a democratic franchise before 1832. In the famous election of 1784 the Duchesses of Devonshire and Portland canvassed for their favourite, Fox. They offered a kiss to every voter promising to vote for Fox. Such treats were forbidden by the Corrupt Practices Act of 1883 – elections are much duller today.

54 Many people benefited from the unreformed and corrupt electoral system before 1832.

changed by the 1832 Reform Act, which gave the vote to tenants who were £10 copyholders, £10 long leaseholders, £50 short leaseholders and tenants paying a rent of £50 a year. [Picture 54]

In the boroughs, as we have seen, the right to vote varied from place to place. By the Reform Act of 1832 the old franchises were abolished and the vote was given to £10 householders – that is the man who owned or rented a property which had been valued by the rating officer as worth £10 a year. We have to remember that money values have changed. In 1832 the Metropolitan Police Force paid its constables 12s 6d per week. Today, the same constables are paid about £25 a week. Taking this as an indication we have to multiply 1832 figures by 40 to get a modern equivalent: this means that the vote was given to people who owned or rented houses valued at the equivalent of £400 a year. As you will see these were very rich men indeed, and it is not surprising that even after this Reform Act only about 650,000 men were allowed to vote.

Persuading the voter

In the nineteenth century, even after the 1832 Reform Act, there was still an open system of voting. This open system of voting on the hustings might have lasted as many as six or seven days in a constituency [Chapter 3, Picture 11]. Throughout this time the various candidates would have hired bands to process through the town, to try and whip up support from those who hadn't voted [Chapter 7, Picture 52]. These bands would be followed by gangs of people – some paid for the purpose – who would cheer or boo the voter according to how he cast his vote. We know of many cases where the gangs threw an unfortunate voter into the pond, or otherwise threatened him, in an effort to 'persuade' people who had not voted.

The candidates and their agents would also be busy trying to persuade the voters to give them their support. In some cases this was a matter of a straightforward money bribe; in other cases it was a promise to do some favour for the voter. In many instances the local landlord or employer could threaten people with dismissals or eviction if they didn't vote as he wanted. [Chapter 3, Picture 12]

Chartism

The 1832 Reform Act was a great disappointment to people who had hoped that the old electoral system would be swept away and that a fully democratic system would be set up so that the ordinary people would have a say in the electing of MPs and so have a chance to exert influence on the government. The Chartists [Picture 55] hoped that if there were a working class electorate that the government would be forced to pass laws about factory conditions, unemployment, housing, food prices and so on. Their attempts to persuade the government to bring in more reforms after 1832 failed; sometimes this failure led to violence, as when

The Six Points
OF THE
PEOPLE'S
CHARTER.

1. A VOTE for every man twenty-one years of age, of sound mind, and not undergoing punishment for crime.

2. THE BALLOT.—To protect the elector in the exercise of his vote.

3. No PROPERTY QUALIFICATION for Members of Parliament —thus enabling the constituencies to return the man of their choice, be he rich or poor.

4. PAYMENT OF MEMBERS, thus enabling an honest trades-man, working man, or other person, to serve a constituency, when taken from his business to attend to the interests of the country.

5. EQUAL CONSTITUENCIES, securing the same amount of representation for the same number of electors, instead of allowing small constituencies to swamp the votes of large ones.

6. ANNUAL PARLIAMENTS, thus presenting the most effectual check to bribery and intimidation, since though a constituency might be bought once in seven years (even with the ballot), no purse could buy a constituency (under a system of universal suffrage) in each ensuing twelvemonth; and since members, when elected for a year only, would not be able to defy and betray their constituents as now.

55   A handbill with the Chartists' demands.

some Chartists rioted at Newport in 1839 and the army was called out to fire on the crowd which was trying to seize the gaol and release Chartist prisoners. The last fling of the Chartists was in 1848 when a mammoth march from Kennington (near the present Surrey Cricket Ground) to Westminster, took a petition signed by over two million people, asking the government to agree to the Chartist demands. This petition was accepted by the House of Commons, but no legislation followed until 1867 when the Conservative government, with the support of many Liberal MPs (including Gladstone), brought in the Second Reform Act which gave the vote to every adult male householder in the boroughs. This gave the vote to about two million men, most of them being skilled workers who had enough money to be able to rent a whole house. It did not give the vote to men sharing a house with another family, so that the poorer workers who lived in overcrowded slums did not yet get the vote. Nor did the over twenty-one-year-old children of the householder get a vote.

This increase in the number of voters meant that the MPs and candidates could not so easily bribe people, although there is plenty of evidence that many employers used their positions to force their men to vote for a particular candidate or lose their jobs. This was stopped by the Ballot Act of 1872, which allowed men to vote in secret for the first time. [Chapter 7, Picture 48]

However, there was still adequate evidence of bribery and 'treating', by which the candidates supplied voters with beer and food in an effort to persuade them to cast their votes 'in the right way'. This was stopped by the Corrupt Practices Act, 1883, which laid down how much money could be spent by a candidate and said *how* it could be spent. Any candidate who spent more than this amount or who was found guilty of spending it in an illegal way was, if elected, to lose his seat.

Towards democracy

In 1884 Parliament passed the Third Reform Act which gave the vote to all adult male householders in the county seats. This was followed in 1885 by an Act which redistributed the constituencies so that the growing towns got more seats and the less densely populated counties lost some of theirs. After 1886 over six million men had the right to vote. Although the country was not yet even a male democracy, it had moved a long way from the corrupt system of the early part of the century when the landowners had dominated the political scene. Now the majority of voters were working-class people and governments either had to pass laws which helped to make their lives better or had to see the growth of a new political party representing the working classes [Picture 56].

Women

However, even as late as 1914 few politicians thought that women ought to have the right to vote. Women were regarded as second class citizens in nineteenth-century Britain. Until 1882 no married woman was allowed to own property: until 1919 no woman could become a graduate of a University or become a lawyer: until 1914 few middle class girls went to work – although working class girls and women still continued to work in engineering works, the coal industry, textile mills and brickyards.

The middle class politicians thought that the woman's place was in the home and not in the office, factory or shop. However, by the end of the nineteenth century there were 'bold' women who had become doctors, followed Florence Nightingale to become nurses, were using the new typewriters and telephones in offices, and working in the new and large shops in London and the main towns.

These more educated and independent women thought that they should have the same rights as men. They could already vote in elections for school boards: they could be elected as Poor Law Guardians – but they could not vote for an MP. Some of these women tried to win their case by peaceful demonstration and pamphlets. Others, led by Mrs Pankhurst, were more violent. They inter-

56 A contemporary cartoonist's view of the 1868 Parliamentary election in Sheffield, where, during the early 1860s, some crucial things had been happening. Now A. J. Mundella, a pro-trade-union hosiery manifacture, was adopted, with Sheffield Trades Council's backing, as Liberal candidate – thus displacing J. A. Roebuck, the anti-trade-union Liberal MP for Sheffield, who had been serving as a member of the Royal Commission of Inquiry into Trade Unions.

57 A procession of arrested Suffragettes walking through St James's Park, London, after an attack on Buckingham Palace, 1914. The little girl (left) later enjoyed the freedom of a vote for which these women were campaigning.

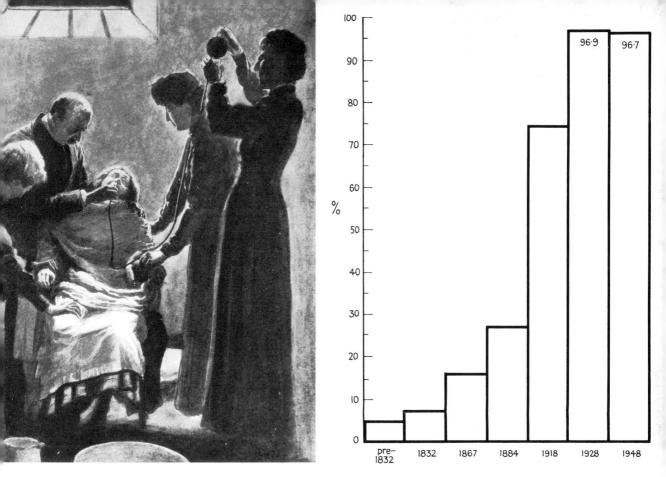

58 *Left* The forcible feeding of a Suffragette prisoner who had gone on hunger strike in 1912.

59 *Right* the apparent reduction of the proportion of adults with the vote in 1948 is explained by the abolition of plural voting.

rupted political meetings, chained themselves to railings in Downing Street and at Buckingham Palace, and allowed themselves to be arrested – to draw attention to their case. They were the first of the 'urban guerrillas' in one sense and they were arrested, ill-treated in prison by the authorities who wanted to squash this 'nonsense' [Picture 58].

1918

However, by 1918, the politicians had been forced to realise that women could play an equal part alongside men – in factories and in the Services, in offices and in government departments. Their contribution to the war effort made politicians change their minds and give the vote to women in 1918 – or at least to give the vote to some women. For, while the 1918 Act gave the vote to all men over the age of twenty-one (so that for the first time Britain was a male democracy) it gave the vote only to women over the age of thirty when, presumably, they had become the equal of a twenty-one-year-old man. This illogicality was ended in 1928 when women were given equal voting rights with men. [Picture 59]

60 13 March 1970: Susan Wallace, who was eighteen on 10 February 1970 makes history as Britain's first schoolgirl voter in a by-election at Bridgewater in Somerset.

1969

Throughout the nineteenth century the right to vote was tied up with the owner-ship of property in one way or other. Even when the second and third Reform Acts gave the vote to some adult working class males, it was on the grounds that they were householders, paying rent and rates. When Britain became a democratic society in 1928 the vote was given to all people over the age of twenty-one – because that was the age at which people could legally own property, become liable for debts, make agreements with hire purchase companies and so on. Even in 1928, then, the vote was linked with the idea of property.

In the 1960s it became clear that Britain's post-war children, brought up in a Welfare State where their parents enjoyed, on the whole, a continually rising standard of living, were healthier than the children of the past. There was also clear evidence that they were better educated, and so support grew for the idea that since people could join the Services, get married, take a job, etc., at the age of eighteen, then perhaps they had the right to vote. Two separate Com-missions were set up to consider the position of Britain's teenagers and as a result of the evidence produced by these Commissions, a series of legal changes were effected which altered the laws concerning property. One of the by-products of these Commissions was that the government decided to lower the voting age to allow eighteen-year-olds to vote [Picture 60] and while a number did so in by-elections in 1969, the first General Election in which these new voters went to the polls was that of 1970.

9 The Prime Minister

Downing Street

One of the world's best known front doors is Number 10 Downing Street. [Picture 61] There can be few people who have not seen a Press photograph or a television film of the doorway through which pass the world's leading statesmen, trade union leaders, business men and financiers on their way to see the British Prime Minister. Number 10 Downing Street has been the official home of the Prime Minister since George I gave the house to Sir Robert Walpole who was his Chief Minister from 1721 to 1742. Next door, in Number 11, lives the Chancellor of the Exchequer. Across the street is the Foreign Office. This short street is one of the most important centres of government in the world.

The front of Number 10 is not very imposing looking, while the back [Picture 63] is equally ordinary looking. Inside, however, there are several very large and beautiful rooms, one of them being the Cabinet Room [Picture 62] where the

61 *Left* Number 10 Downing Street, the home of the Prime Minister and the scene of Cabinet meetings.

62 *Right* the Cabinet Room in Number 10 Downing Street.

Prime Minister sits as chairman during meetings of his Cabinet. He will invite his Ministers to give their opinion on the subject under discussion. When they have all had their say, he sums up and announces that the feeling of the Cabinet is so-and-so. This, then, becomes the government policy on that issue. Any Minister has the freedom to disagree inside the Cabinet Room, but, unless he resigns from the Cabinet, he is bound to support the decision. In speeches, articles, interviews or answers in Parliament, the Ministers will all give the impression that they agree with whatever decisions have been made in the Cabinet Room.

The Eighteenth Century
As we have seen (Chapter 2) the number of professional party politicians was very small in the eighteenth century. These few tended to group themselves around one or other of the more important politicians – so that there were Grafton Whigs, Foxites, Rockingham Whigs and so on. In this situation a Prime Minister was truly described as 'primus inter pares' – the first among equals. The politicians knew that one of their number had to be chairman at Cabinet Meetings and had to carry reports of their meetings to the King. But they treated this chairman as only one of themselves and not someone especially set apart and different. Before Walpole became Prime Minister in 1721 there was a bewildering series of changes of Chief Ministers as Carteret, Pulteney and Townshend swopped jobs. In the thirty years after Walpole's resignation there were many Prime Ministers, few of whom governed for very long.

Nineteenth-century Prime Ministers
It is interesting to note that as late as the eighteenth century we divide the history of England up into the reigns of monarchs. Starting with Queen Anne, students are taken through the reigns of George I and George II. The accession

of George III is often taken as the starting point for a new period of history. But in the nineteenth century we study the work of Ministries, of Grey and Melbourne, Peel and Palmerston and, above all, Gladstone and Disraeli. The accession of Queen Victoria in 1837 and her death in 1901 are less important than the fall of Gladstone in 1874 or the defeat of the Tories in 1906.

In the middle of the nineteenth century a Prime Minister (e.g. Peel or Russell) was an important figure but, as the history of the period shows, other politicians could challenge their power and sometimes defeat them. Thus Palmerston having been dismissed as Foreign Minister in 1851, organised the defeat and dismissal of his Prime Minister, Russell, in 1852. By the end of the nineteenth century party discipline was tighter and the power of the Prime Minister was greater so that Salisbury was able to resist the challenge of Lord Randolph Churchill, while Gladstone defeated Chamberlain's attempts to seize the leadership in 1886 (Chapter 6). Richard Cobden had been able to lead Peel along the road to Free Trade in 1846 but Chamberlain was unable to lead Balfour back down that road in 1904. [Chapter 5, Picture 28]

As party discipline became stronger so the power of the Prime Minister increased, so that the Prime Minister has become, as it were, an uncrowned King. Two Prime Ministers have tried to use their power to try and break with the Party system. One of them, Lloyd George was the advocate of the New Liberalism [Chapter 3, Picture 16] and the enemy of the Conservatives in 1909 [Chapter 5, Picture 31]. But even then Lloyd George thought that –

> we were beset by an accumulation of grave issues – rapidly become graver. . . . It was becoming evident to discerning eyes that the party and parliamentary system was unequal to coping with them.

From his home in Criccieth he wrote a memorandum:

> urging that a truce should be declared between the parties for the purpose of securing the cooperation of the leading party statesmen in a settlement of our national problems – second chamber, home rule, the development of our agricultural resources, national training for defence, the remedying of social evils, and a fair and judicial inquiry into the working of our fiscal system.

In 1916, supported by some Liberals and many Conservatives, Lloyd George overthrew Asquith and led his Coalition government to a great victory in the 1918 Election, when he had a majority of over 400 over the Asquithian Liberals and the small Labour Party. The former Liberal champion then tried to set up a new Party. Ninety-five members of Parliament, gathered together by Captain Colin Coote, sent to Lloyd George and Bonar Law a message:

> that this group, believing in the national necessity for the coalition, expresses the hope that it may develop into a single united party.

Balfour drafted for his constituency chairman a letter, intended for publication, strongly advocating fusion. He showed it to Bonar Law, who consulted Lloyd George, and with Bonar Law's agreement Lloyd George decided to test the feelings of Coalition Liberal members. To his surprise he found that they were anxious to keep their identity and the Liberal name.

But his attempt to remain Prime Minister meant that this party-less leader had to keep on changing policies:

To keep the seat of power, the place of patronage, [Lord Beaverbrook says], he was prepared to stand out as the leader of Empire-minded men – or appear as the Liberal Apostle of Free Trade; as the Man of Peace in Europe – or the Man of War against Turkey and France; as the hammer of the Russian Bolsheviks – or their noble conciliator as the Tribune of the British working classes – or the Champion of the Tory landlords against Labour: stern enemy of the Irish – or their tender friend spreading his covering wings about another Celtic race ground under the heel of the oppressor. He took up each position in turn during those tragic years of 1921 and 1922.

64 Prime Minister Ramsay MacDonald trying to mix up the Parties to form a Coalition.

65 The quiet leader of the social revolution, 1945–51, Clement Attlee.

In 1922 the Conservatives withdrew their support from Lloyd George, who had to resign, to be followed by Bonar Law and later by Stanley Baldwin. [Picture 63]

The other Prime Minister who tried to escape from the Party machine was Ramsay MacDonald. In 1931 he was Prime Minister for the second time. He realised that his government did not have a majority in the Commons so that it was unable to cope with the problems following the economic crisis which swept the world following the Wall Street crash [Picture 64]. He formed a Coalition government [Chapter 4, Picture 24] in the hope that this new government would be able to hit upon solutions. The 1931 Election showed that the majority of the MPs returned to the Commons were Conservatives and in 1935 MacDonald resigned to make way for Baldwin.

Post-war Prime Ministers

Clement Attlee led a strong Labour government in 1945 [Picture 65]. He believed it was his job to allow his Ministers to run their own departments while he acted as a sort of chairman at Cabinet meetings. However, he also showed that he had the power to dismiss even the strongest Ministers when he thought they were no longer up to their jobs.

His successors in both Labour and Conservative governments have used the same sort of power. Harold Macmillan became leader of the Conservatives in 1957 [Picture 66]. In July 1962 he dismissed half his Cabinet in the hope that new faces in the Cabinet Room would lead to new policies and support from the electors. Harold Wilson, as Labour Prime Minister, warned his Labour colleagues that his electoral success in 1966 had given the individual MP a licence to attend the Commons, and just as dog licences could be taken away, so could the MPs' licences. Neither Macmillan nor Wilson had to face any real challenge to their leadership from fellow Ministers, in spite of their actions and language [Picture 67].

Prime Ministers' power

The basis of the Prime Minister's power lies in the fact that the mass electorate, taking their politics from the mass media of Press and TV, now sees the party

" Marvellous! My popularity among the passengers isn't sinking ! "

contest as a fight between Party leaders. The Parties concentrate their publicity on the Party leaders. MPs are elected to support a leader. If they hesitate to do so the Party Whips guide them with the stick of discipline or the carrot of patronage; only 'good' MPs are chosen to become Ministers. Ministers know that they can be replaced whenever the Prime Minister so decides – this makes them quite willing to follow his lead. In 1966 one Labour MP in three was a member of the Wilson government, while another one-third must have been hoping to be chosen the next time round.

Uncrowned Kings

Modern Prime Ministers have become the real head of the government in a way that would have seemed strange, even to the Younger Pitt in 1804. George III and Bolingbroke [Chapter 2, Picture 8] would find the present position incredible since this is not what the Glorious Revolution of 1688 intended. The first party politicians intended to try to gain control of the Parliament and government so that they could persuade the King to follow a particular line. In the late twentieth century we have replaced the power of the Crown with the power of the Prime Minister.

66 *Opposite above,* Lord Hailsham speaking during the 1959 Election. The posters show the importance which modern Parties attach to the Party Leader. Prime Minister Macmillan's portrait dominates the room. Politicians know that people vote *against* rather than for, so they emphasise the weaknesses of the other Party.

67 *Opposite below,* leading Labour Ministers – George Brown (centre) and Jim Callaghan (right) – wanted to devalue the pound in 1966. The Party Leader, Harold Wilson refused to do so – and they followed his lead.

10 The Changing Nature of the Modern Conservative and Labour Parties

Changes in parties

We have seen that political parties are formed by people who wish to gain control of Parliament and the government so that they can decide what laws should or should not be passed. In the seventeenth and eighteenth centuries only the rich had a say in the government of the country, so that only the rich helped to form the early political parties. When the middle classes were given the vote in 1832 they, too, joined in the political contest while working men became involved only after they had been given the vote in 1867. The aristocratic leaders of the early political parties had to make way for the middle class leaders – such as Joseph Chamberlain and Richard Cobden.

In the twentieth century working men such as Ernest Bevin have made their way to the top of the political tree [Picture 68].

Party aims

However, it is not only the membership and the leadership of political parties that has changed as time has gone on. There has also had to be a change in the

68 Ernest Bevin in 1920 when he was a leader of the Dockers' Union (now part of the Transport and General Workers' Union). During the Second World War Winston Churchill invited Bevin to join his government as Minister of Labour; in the Attlee Government of 1945 he was Foreign Secretary.

69 The Attlee Government wanted to create a Welfare State, which led to an increase in taxation. The same government also began a massive rearmament programme costing £1,500 million a year, which led to more increases in taxation. Many socialists though that the rearmament was a betrayal of socialist principles.

"ALL I ASK IS THAT YOU GET IT PROPERLY BALANCED"

aims of the parties. The politicians of the seventeenth and eighteenth centuries were anxious to curb the power of the King, and to make sure that the Catholic Stuarts did not return to the throne of this country. The middle class politicians of the mid-nineteenth century wanted laws passed about trade and industry. The working class politicians of the twentieth century wanted laws passed about housing and unemployment.

The changing Labour Party

The form of a political party and the nature of its aims changes in response to changes in the economic and social framework of the country. Gladstone [Chapter 5, Picture 27], would have thought that Lloyd George [Chapter 5, Picture 33] was a socialist. It is equally doubtful whether the early leaders of the Independent Labour Party would recognise the modern Labour Party. In its origins, the Labour Party contained two groups: there were the socialists (of the Independent Labour Party and the Fabian Society) who wanted to get laws passed to 'nationalise the means of distribution, production and exchange', to provide free education for people at school, colleges and universities, to provide pensions for the old and unemployment benefit for the workless. Then there were the trade unions which linked with the socialists after 1900; they wanted to get laws passed which would safeguard the position of trade unions and get better wages for lowly paid workers.

The Attlee governments [Picture 69]

During the 1930s the Labour Party campaigned for better treatment for the millions of unemployed; it continued to argue that a socialist state could be created in Britain and that in such a state life would be better. In 1945 the Attlee government had a chance to put Labour's ideas into practice – and indeed, life is much better as a result of the creation of the Welfare State. But the Attlee

87

70 *Left* A major reason for the Labour Party's growth in the 1920s was the inability of the Conservatives to deal with the problem of unemployment. In the full employment of the 1950s and 1960s this ceased to be an important issue.

71 *Right* The old leader (Attlee) shaking hands with the new (Wilson) as a new era begins for the Labour Party, as it again tried to show that it was not merely a Party of protest but a Party of government.

government was also forced to recognise that a completely socialist state could not be created. While many industries were nationalised, many important industries were left in the hands of the private enterprise capitalists – whom previous Labour writers and speakers had attacked as enemies of the working class. The Attlee government had to learn how to run an economy in which some things were done by the government and some things done by the capitalists.

In 1951 the Conservatives came back into power and proved in the next thirteen years that they too could run a mixed economy and could continue to develop the Welfare State. Indeed in the 1959 election Prime Minister Macmillan argued that the affluent society was the creation of the Conservative governments and that the Labour Party would ruin it [Chapter 9, Picture 67]. If the Conservatives could run a mixed economy and make life better for the majority of the British people, what was left for the Labour Party? In its early days it had promised to create a socialist society; when in power it had been forced to realise that this could not be done. In the early days it had been able to argue, with some justification, that the Conservatives could not make life better: by 1959 this was obviously untrue. Anything that Labour could do, the Conservatives could do – and, it seemed, to do better [Picture 70].

The Wilson era

In 1963 Harold Wilson became leader of the Labour Party. He had been a member of the Attlee Cabinet in 1947 and knew that in the changing economic and social scene of the 1960s the Labour Party could not expect to win power if it merely offered again to make 'life better' or to 'end unemployment'. New issues had to be found, new ideas had to be presented if the Labour Party was to win. Mr Wilson argued that while the Conservatives could run an affluent society, they did it badly; he also argued that because most Conservative leaders were rich they did not understand the hopes of the increasing number of young, qualified and ambitious people coming out of universities and colleges. In effect, Wilson claimed that the Labour Party was better suited than the Conservatives to take Britain through the technological revolution of the 1960s and 1970s. [Picture 73]

In 1964 and 1966 his ideas appealed to the electorate and he had seven years in which to prove that the Labour Party could govern in the late twentieth century. During this period his government made many fundamental changes in the economic and social life of the country; the steel industry was re-nationalised: firms in the engineering, motor car and shipbuilding industries were encouraged to group themselves into larger and fewer firms; the country's Balance of Payments was brought from a position where we spent more than we earned to one where we earned a huge surplus.

But for many socialists all this was irrelevant. Was it the duty of a Labour Government to force firms such as English Electric and General Electric to become more competitive and larger? Was the creation of British Leyland something that a Labour Government should be proud of? Wilson's critics argued that the Conservatives had done just this with the aircraft industry in the 1950s, when they had forced every firm in the aircraft building industry to join one or other of two larger firms. It seemed to many people that the only argument in favour of a Labour Government was that it would do the same sort of things as a Conservative government would have done – and to socialists this was not a good argument [Picture 75].

Meanwhile, in other ways, the Labour government was showing itself to be 'the best Conservative government the country has had'. A strict wages freeze was enforced by a Prices and Incomes Board; trade unions were threatened with a Bill aimed at weakening their power; fewer houses were built, while over £2,000 million continued to be spent on rearmament every year. For many socialists all these things were wrong and certainly the opposite of what they expected a Labour government to do.

The middle ground

One way of thinking about the electorate in the twentieth century is to see it as a line of people. At one end are those who believe in a completely communist

72 Labour's George Brown introduced a 'Prices and Incomes' policy as part of the government's programme to modernise Britain in the 1960s. The policy had little success and was very unpopular with the Party's supporters in the country.

society; at the other end those who believe in a society in which the government would behave as nineteenth-century governments had done, when nothing was done for the poor, the homeless or the old. If you think about the electorate as such a line you will realise that in the middle of the line is a group of voters who are not quite sure which way they really want to go; sometimes, and on some issues, they may want the government to take action; on some other issues and at some other times they think the government should not act. These voters occupy what politicians call the 'middle ground'. And there are an increasing number of such voters.

The Conservative Party knows that it can almost always call on the support of the people at one end of the line. The Labour Party knows that it can expect the support of the people at the other end of the line who want the government to become more active. In the 1960s and 1970s the political struggle between the two parties has been about the voters in the middle. Which of the two parties will they support? In 1964 and 1966 they supported the Labour Party; in 1970 they supported the Conservatives.

If the Labour Party wishes to win power it has to satisfy its own regular supporters that it is a party committed to making the government more active in matters of housing, education, pensions and so on. However, it has also to win the support of the middle ground and show that it can run a modern economy and tackle such problems as inflation, trade union militancy and so on. There is a real problem here for Labour leaders because if they prove very good socialists they may lose the middle ground, but if they satisfy the middle ground they may lose the support of their regular voters who, by abstaining from voting, can allow the Conservatives to win elections.

73 The Conservatives government under Prime Minister Macmillan was forced to adopt many socialist ideas – such as economic planning. Harold Wilson, then leader of the Opposition, is seen overtaking the Chancellor of the Exchequer, Selwyn Lloyd – on his way to power as the man who was going to use planning more extensively and wisely than the Conservatives had done. By 1970 his reputation was also in shreds.

The changing nature of the Modern Conservatives

In the 1920s and 1930s Stanley Baldwin [Chapter 9, Picture 63] led the Conservative Party away from being a right wing, nineteenth-century party opposed to the introduction of the Welfare State, so that it became a liberal-minded Party providing governments which, in the 1920s and 1930s, did a great deal to develop the Welfare State. However, the Conservative governments were unable to do very much for the millions of unemployed, and memories of the depressed 1930s were among the reasons for the surprising defeat of Churchill and the Conservatives in 1945.

In the mid 1950s, under Harold Macmillan, the Conservative Party showed that it was quite prepared to run an economy in which some industries were owned by the state and some owned by private capitalists; they too, it seemed, could be as good as the Attlee government. They also showed that they wanted life to be better for the majority of people; they, like the Attlee government, continued to maintain a high level of employment and allowed trade unions to get high wages for their members, who enjoyed a high standard of living [Picture 74].

The Macmillan governments also showed that they realised that Britain lived in the mid-twentieth century by recognising the claims to independence of a large number of African countries which had once been part of the British

91

74 Prime Minister Macmillan addressing the members of the South African Parliament. His 'wind of change' speech put the Conservatives on the side of the liberal and radical opponents of apartheid.

Empire. Conservatives, too – it seemed – were the friends of former colonial peoples. Harold Macmillan took the opportunity of a trip to South Africa to warn the South African government that a 'wind of change' was blowing through Africa and that a policy of white supremacy was doomed to fail. Conservatives, it seemed, were as righteous as socialists.

The Heath government

In the elections of 1959, 1964 and 1966 the contest between the two main parties was not about major principles; both seemed to be agreed on these; both believed in a mixed economy, both believed in the Welfare State, more and better housing, schooling and treatment for the old and sick. Many people thought of the two parties as Tweedledum and Tweedledee.

However, in the election of 1970 the Conservatives took a distinctly different line to the Labour Party, a line which was also different from that which had been taken by previous Conservative governments. For the first time for many years they argued that the government should do less – for the sick – who would have to pay a higher share of the cost of their medicine; for schoolchildren – who would have to pay a higher price for school meals. By doing less, taxes could be cut so that life could be made better for people who had been paying high taxes.

This is a reversal of Conservative policy followed since Baldwin's time, and marks a shift to the right as compared with the continued shift to the left which previous Conservative governments have shown. In the last thirty years the battle between the two main parties has been about the middle ground. Now the battle is between two parties, one of which has swung away to the right. The other may still continue to battle for the abandoned middle ground, or it may indeed, swing away to the left. Certainly the nature of the aims of the political parties will once again change [Picture 75].

THE PEN AND THE SWORD

75 If the Heath government has taken a swing to the right and away from the middle ground some people expect the Labour Party to take a swing to the left and towards a more socialist policy.

Further Reading

General studies of the history of political parties can be found in:
1. *The Growth of the British Party System* Ivor Bulmer Thomas
2. *British Political Parties* R. T. Mackenzie
3. *British Political Parties: Vol. 2 The Growth of Parties* Sir Ivor Jennings

Histories of the different parties can be traced in:
1. *The Liberal Party* J. S. Rasmussen
2. *The Liberal Party from Earl Grey to Asquith* R. B. McCallum
3. *The Downfall of the Liberal Party* T. Wilson
4. *A History of the Tory Party 1640–1714* K. Feiling
5. *A History of the Second Tory Party 1714–1832* K. Feiling
6. *British Conservatism 1832–1914* R. B. McDowell
7. *A Short History of the Labour Party* H. Pelling

Documentary material is readily available in the series *British Political Tradition*:

1. *The Conservative Tradition* (ed.) R. J. White
2. *The Liberal Tradition* (eds.) Bullock and Shock
3. *The Challenge of Socialism* (ed.) H. Pelling
4. *The English Radical Tradition* (ed.) S. Maccoby

The autobiographies of recent politicians throw some light on the more recent turns. Among the more readable are:

1. *Memoirs* Herbert Morrison
2. *A Prime Minister Remembers* C. R. Attlee (ed.) Francis Williams
3. *The Greasy Pole* R. Bevins
4. *Autobiography* Philip Snowden
5. Volumes of memoirs, Hugh Dalton
6. Volumes of memoirs, Harold Macmillan
7. Volumes of memoirs, Lord Avon (Anthony Eden)

There are biographies of almost every famous politician. Among these are:

1. *Wilkes and Liberty* G. Rudé
2. *Salisbury*, Kennedy
3. *Lord Randolph Churchill* R. R. James
4. *The Unknown Prime Minister* (Bonar Law), R. Blake
5. *Disraeli* R. Blake
6. *Gladstone* Sir Philip Magnus
7. *Chilston Chief Whip*, Chilston
8. *A Life for Unity* (J. H. Thomas), Blaxland
9. *Victorian People* Asa Briggs

Political issues are dealt with in:

1. *Votes for Women* Roger Fulford
2. *Balfour's Poodle* (1909–12), Roy Jenkins
3. *The Elected Monarch* (on the Prime Minister's power), F. W. G. Benemy

The nature of local party associations can be studied in:
    Voters Parties and Leaders J. Blondel (Penguin)

Novels are a useful aid to the student. Among those which are a help in this present context are:

1. *Tom Jones* (on the eighteenth-century Tory Squire), Henry Fielding
2. *The Rape of a Fair Country* and *Rebecca's Daughters* (on industrial development in Wales and the spread of Chartism), A. Cordell
3. *Fame is the Spur* (which tells of Peterloo and the growth of a Radical movement), Howard Spring
4. *Sybil* and *Coningsby* (on the need for a new Tory Party), B. Disraeli

Index

The numbers in **bold** type indicate the page numbers where illustrations occur.